THE UNITY OF THE NATIONS

JOSEPH RATZINGER

(POPE BENEDICT XVI)

THE UNITY OF THE NATIONS

A VISION OF THE CHURCH FATHERS

TRANSLATED BY BONIFACE RAMSEY

THE CATHOLIC UNIVERSITY OF AMERICA PRESS
WASHINGTON, D.C.

Originally published in German as *Die Einheit der Nationen:*
Eine Vision der Kirchenväter
Licensed by Verlag Anton Pustet, Salzburg, Austria
German text © Libreria Editrice Vaticana. © 2005 Verlag
Anton Pustet. All rights reserved.
The paper used in this publication meets the minimum
requirements of American National Standards for
Information Science—Permanence of Paper for Printed
Library Materials, ANSI Z39.48-1984.
∞

Design and typesetting by Kachergis Book Design

Library of Congress Cataloging-in-Publication Data
Benedict XVI, Pope, 1927–
[Einheit der Nationen. English]
The unity of the nations : a vision of the church fathers
/ Joseph Ratzinger (Pope Benedict XVI) ; translated by
Boniface Ramsey.
pages cm
Includes bibliographical references and index.
ISBN 978-0-8132-2723-8 (pbk. : alk. paper)   1. Christianity
and politics—History.   2. Origen.   3. Augustine, Saint,
Bishop of Hippo.   I. Title.
BR115.P7R42613 2015
261.7—dc23   2014043405

CONTENTS

TRANSLATOR'S NOTE

Father Joseph Ratzinger, as he was known at the time, mentions in the Preface that this book presents a lecture that he gave in Salzburg in 1962 and finally published in book form in 1970. He did not believe that after eight years there was any pressing need to update his original references, and I do not believe that after more than fifty years I have the right to make an important change of that sort unilaterally. In the notes, however, I have offered English translations of the passages that he quoted in Origen's Greek and Augustine's Latin. I have usually relied on extant translations and have cited the translators, but in the few cases where I have done the translation myself, no translator is named. Also, rather than relegate such explanations to the footnotes (which would have meant changing their original numbering), I have very occasionally, and I hope as unobtrusively as possible, supplemented Father Ratzinger's text when I felt that a reader today would find that useful, as on page 6, where I added a few words about "Ocean." Finally, I have consistently translated *das Nationale*, which appears frequently in the original German, as "national identity."

Quotes from Augustine, *The City of God*, trans. W. Babcock, *The Works of Saint Augustine* I/6 and I/7 (Hyde Park, N.Y.: New City Press, 2012–13), © Augustinian Heritage Institute, are used with permission.

On April 18, 2008, Joseph Ratzinger, then Pope Benedict XVI, presided at an ecumenical service at St. Joseph's Church–Yorkville on the occasion of his pastoral visit to New York. As the present pastor of St. Joseph's, I wish to acknowledge the warm bond between now Pope Emeritus Benedict XVI and our parish and also to thank my parishioners for allowing me the time to translate his book. I dedicate this translation to them.

BONIFACE RAMSEY

FOREWORD TO THE
GERMAN EDITION (2005)

Does what is Christian have a place in the political world? This is one of the issues that Anton Pustet's Transformation series is concerned with exploring.* By the very act of choosing his name, Pope Benedict XVI wanted to confront this question: at the moment of his election, as the new apostle of the western world, Joseph Ratzinger embraced as his goal the religious "re-education" of that world. His essay on the unity of the nations, which we present afresh after the passage of several decades, has something of an anticipatory feel to it in that respect. Using the examples of the Christian thinkers Origen and Augustine, Ratzinger

*Published by Verlag Anton Pustet, Salzburg.

shows what a great revolutionary awareness there was in early Christianity. For him the nations in question were mere artificial constructs that were incomplete apart from the contribution provided by a universal sense of the human. Joseph Weiler's essay, "A Christian Europe," which opened the Transformation series, is organically connected to Ratzinger's. Weiler, a believing Jew and a jurist who specializes in European law, observes that, in the Europe which is currently being formed, its overwhelmingly Christian history is subject to an astonishing neglect. Perhaps precisely in such a context, Christianity, understood in a universal sense, can inspire that supranational ethic which cannot emerge solely from the sphere of politics or economics.

MONA MÜRY-LEITNER

PREFACE

The following chapters represent the text of a lecture that the author gave in the fall of 1962 during the Salzburg University Weeks. A short excerpt was published at the time in the journal of the Catholic Academic Association, *Der katholische Gedanke* 19 (1963): 1–9. A longer portion had already been printed before that in *Studium Generale* 14 (1961): 664–82. A comprehensive investigation of the relationship between national and human identity according to the mind of the Church Fathers could obviously not be my goal in the space that was allotted to me. What I aimed at was simply to sketch out a few of the main aspects of the problem, using the two great figures of Origen and Augustine as examples. Meanwhile this issue has gained significance in particular because of the ever-expanding discussion of political theology. Since neither of the newspapers in which the Salzburg lecture was published at the time had a wide circulation, I decided, for the sake not only of those who were interested in the Fathers but also of those who were engaged in the conversation about political theology, to act on Dr. Lampey's kind encouragement and publish the essay in its entirety in the *Bibliothek der Salzburger Hochschulwochen*, for which Dr. Lampey has been responsible for many years. I am unaware of the results of any research over the past few years that would necessitate factual changes in my presentation, and the mere addition of new publications, which can easily be found in current bibliographies, does not make sense to me. For this reason the lecture that I gave then is essentially unchanged. I hope that, precisely as such, it can contribute to today's conversation.

JOSEPH RATZINGER
Regensburg
November 15, 1970

THE
UNITY
OF THE
NATIONS

1

THE INTELLECTUAL AND SPIRITUAL BACKGROUND OF THE QUESTION

The Heritage of Antiquity

Early Christianity's struggle for its precise place in the political world, which will be explored in the following reflections by focusing on some particular details, is decisively marked by three components: most important, first of all, was biblical faith; next, the heritage of Antiquity necessarily had an effect; and, finally, the debate with so-called gnosis and its reception of the Christian message played a major role.

For our purposes it will have to suffice to make a rough sketch of this tripartite background. We may begin with the heritage of Antiquity, which should in no way be thought of monolithically—not even in the period of so-called universal Hellenistic culture. It is true that this culture led to a melding of countless elements of tradition and thus created something like a single intellectual language, yet it was dissipated in a multiplicity of directions and paths. With respect to the issue that we are dealing with, two opposed currents are more important than any others: the first of these is what could be designated the political theology of the Roman Empire, and then there is what has been called the philosophical opposition.[1] Behind the difference of cultural forms Stoicism had discovered the unity of the being "man," the unvarying humanity of man, which exists throughout all times and places. It had discovered that the entire *cosmos* was nothing other than Zeus's immense body and that all of humankind was a single body.[2] But the consequences that were drawn from this were actually quite different. Antisthenes and his disciple Diogenes saw in this the apolitical-

1. For these necessarily brief and very summary thoughts I have relied especially on A. A. T. Ehrhardt, *Politische Metaphysik von Solon bis Augustin* I/II (Tübingen, 1959); III (Tübingen, 1969). For the political theology of Rome see especially ibid., I, 256–309, and for the "philosophical opposition" and also for its closeness to the Christian opposition see ibid., I, 247ff and II, 15–16.

2. See ibid., I, 148; *Theologisches Wörterbuch zum Neuen Testament* VII, 1035ff.

4

individualistic ideal of the world-citizen, who puts himself above the laws of the state or in any event shows them little respect, because what he wants more than anything else is simply to be a "man."[3] This stance of inner freedom vis-à-vis the state aimed not at a political but at an ethical revolution, at changing man rather than changing his relationships. There is no doubt that this provided the Christian opposition with some decisive points of departure and helped pave the way for that inner freedom which allowed Christian martyrs to set their faith-filled conviction over against the authority of the state, the internal strength of truth over against the external force of earthly powers. Yet here a basic new approach made its appearance, as we shall see next.

Let us stay for a moment in the world of Antiquity in order to take note of the fact that the discovery of the unity of all human beings could

---

3. See Ehrhardt, *Politische Metaphysik* I, 147–48, 163.

most certainly become the point of departure for a political philosophy too. This very same philosophical idea is evident as early as the time of Alexander the Great and underlay his political goal of creating an empire that would embrace the *oikumene,* the entire living space of human civilization reaching as far as the boundaries of Ocean, the great body of water that was said by ancient geographers to surround the earth's dry land.[4] Later on, most likely in connection with Aristotle's *Politics,* the idea of a divine monarchy came to the fore, which was concretely realized in the monarchy of the Roman *princeps,* the prince or ruler. Two varieties of divine monarchy can be distinguished. In the Hellenistic realm God appeared as the monarch; he did not rule himself but rather, off in the background, held in his hands the strings of the cosmic puppet theater. He left governance to the different this-worldly guardians to whom he had entrusted

4. On the philosophical background of Alexander's politics see ibid., I, 172–80.

the individual nations. This indicates, on the political level, a strong emphasis on particular national structures and, on the religious level, a new justification for polytheism—that is, for the particular religions of the time, since the one God, the divine monarch, did not actually rule.[5] On the other side of the spectrum from the Hellenistic realm stood Rome, which was concerned with the idea of unity. As already mentioned, the whole world was Zeus's body; the hidden divine unity that characterized the world was converted into political reality by the Roman *princeps.* This is why Augustus saw to it that the goddess of peace was given the characteristics of Mother Earth at his Altar of Peace, the famous Ara Pacis: the peace that he wanted to bring humankind was a cosmic event, the realization of the unity of the body of humankind.[6]

5. For extensive documentation of this see E. Peterson, "Der Monotheismus als politisches Problem," in Peterson, *Theologische Traktate* (Munich, 1951), 45–147.
6. See Ehrhardt, *Politische Metaphysik,* especially I, 295ff.

The Biblical Background

With this we have reached the point where Christian belief and the heritage of Antiquity came into direct contact with one another. According to the description of the evangelist Luke, who was imbued with Hellenistic sensibilities, when Jesus was born there resounded over the fields of Bethlehem the angels' song of praise, which glorified God and proclaimed "peace on earth among men with whom he is pleased" (Lk 2:14). The text's intention here is certainly to portray something quite different than a heartwarmingly idyllic scene. A few years before, between 12 and 9 B.C., Augustus had erected the Ara Pacis and introduced the cult of his new goddess, Peace; the joyful message of his reign praised "peace on earth."[7] In the words of Virgil, the prophet of the Saturnine Age, "This is the man, this is he, who you know was long promised to you, Caesar

7. See ibid., I, 295, 303; II, 27.

Augustus, the son of god and the bringer of the golden age."[8] Rome promised the world a *pax romana*. The unification of humankind, its peace and its well-being were supposed to come thanks to the force of Roman arms and the power of the *princeps*, who embodied the power of eternal Rome. The cosmic claims of the *pax romana* were made clear when the goddess of the Ara Pacis featured the characteristics of Mother Earth.[9]

The cosmic mystique of Rome, which was visible here in the background and was zealously promoted by rhetoricians and court poets,[10] was nourished by old ideas of the cosmic character of the *polis* and by the newer Stoic reflections on the unity of humankind and of the world.[11]

The encounter between Bethlehem's message of

---

8. *Aeneid* 6, 791–93. See E. Stauffer, *Jerusalem und Rom* (Bern, 1957), 27.
9. See Ehrhardt, *Politische Metaphysik* I, 302.
10. See the extensive documentation on this ibid., II, 41ff; also I, 256–309; Stauffer, *Jerusalem und Rome*, 20–39, and note 8.
11. See Ehrhardt, *Politische Metaphysik* I, 146–206.

peace and the Augustan promise of a *pax romana*
had a symptomatic significance for the collision
of the two worlds under discussion in respect to
both their kinship and their profound differences.
The idea of the unity of the world and of humanity
had a firm basis in biblical belief in the acknowledgement of one God and in the fact that all of
history was rooted in the one Adam and then again
in the one patriarch Noah. Furthermore, both
starting points, the unity of God "from above" and
the unity of a common ancestry "from below," were
held together by the understanding of "Adam"—
namely, of man as the image of God (Gn 1:26),
purely and simply, mediated by reflection on the
covenant with Noah; God's covenantal rainbow
spanned the whole earth (Gn 9:12–17) and his providence embraced all people.[12] On the other side,
Hellenistic philosophy had seized upon the Orphic

12. See G. von Rad, *Theologie des Alten Testaments* I (Munich, 1958), 144–
57, 165–68; J. Daniélou, *Die heiligen Heiden des Alten Testaments* (Stuttgart, 1958); J. Ratzinger, *Christliche Brüderlichkeit* (Munich, 1960).

idea that the entire universe was contained in
Zeus's vast body,[13] and from there it thought
through the unity of the divine, the *cosmos*, and
humanity in its own way. The Roman Empire,
however, saw in itself the real-political implemen-
tation out of this idea, and its *princeps* manifested
the divine monarchy on earth.[14]

A basic difference immediately comes to mind:
In Greco-Roman culture the unity of the world
had its source in pantheism; the divine was itself a
part of the world, and the world had divine status.
Hence the unity of humanity could be converted
directly into political reality. There was unity in
the world itself, and so this unity could be realized
within the world and from out of the world's own
resources. The Roman emperor saw himself as the
one who would bring this divine world power into

13. See Proclus, *Commentary on Timaeus* 28c. See Ehrhardt, I, 148.
14. See Peterson, "Der Monotheismus," 45–147, especially 70ff and
86–102, 149–64; Ehrhardt, *Politische Metaphysik* I, 269ff; Stauffer, *Jerusalem*, 36ff, note 8.

being and therefore as the channel connecting the divine and the world of human beings. In the Bible, on the other hand, God stands free vis-à-vis the world. The story of the Tower of Babel in Gn 11:1–10, which follows right after the list of the peoples that points to the unity of all human beings, informs the reader that God punished humanity, which had grown sinful, by breaking it up into a multiplicity of different and mutually incomprehensible languages. The division of humanity is, to be sure, the fault of men, but it is also their punishment and hence not merely something that one day, when they wanted to, they could get themselves out of. The fact that God stands apart in freedom, and that his power is independent of the world, limits the power and possibility of man, who can in no way bring about the unity of the world on his own, since this division was imposed upon him by God's sovereign will. The Old Testament, indeed, constantly looks forward to the moment when all peoples will make their way, pilgrim-like, to Mount

Zion, and when Jerusalem will be the capital and center of a unified humanity, yet it sees this not as a mission that can be carried out in a directly political fashion but rather as an eschatological hope whose accomplishment is, in the last resort, God's doing.[15]

In the New Testament this opposition between the biblical and the Greco-Roman idea of unity was further sharpened by the confrontation of the two-Adams doctrine, featured especially in Rom 5:12–21 and 1 Cor 15:45–49,[16] and the earlier one-Adam doctrine. This led to a further development of the doctrine—which already appears in the Old Testament—of two *poleis*, or cities, that stood in contrast to the Greco-Roman idea of a single *cosmopolis*, or universal city, which at first

15. On the people of all nations making their way to Jerusalem, see J. Jeremias, *Jesu Verheissung für die Völker*, 2nd ed. (Stuttgart, 1959), 48–60. On the hope of Israel, see R. Schnackenburg, *Gottes Herrschaft und Reich* (Freiburg, 1959), 1–47.

16. See O. Cullmann, *Die Christologie des Neuen Testaments* (Tübingen, 1957), 138–98.

implied the identification of that *polis* with the cosmos but later had as a consequence the transferal of the equation *polis = cosmos* to Rome, the one *polis* that dominated the ancient world.[17] The two-Adams doctrine says that humanity in its former condition, when in its entirety it was a single Adam, had no finality to it, that it was wholly marked by its failed beginning, and that hence, as a whole, it was something which needed to be overcome—that is, which needed to pass through death and downfall. It indicates, furthermore, that with Christ, the Crucified and Risen One, there began humanity's second and final phase, into which a person is incorporated not by way of blood descent but rather by being made subject to the death-destiny of the Crucified One—in other words, by overcoming the former merely natural human condition and by embracing the life of the

17. On the idea of a *cosmopolis*, see Ehrhardt, *Politische Metaphysik* I, 151ff, and on its eventually being understood as the Roman Empire, see ibid., I, 198ff, 227–28; II, 126.

new "second" humanness of the incarnate God, which unmasks as false the humanness that merely divinizes itself.[18]

The community of Christian believers claims to be this second and final humanity, which even now is being built upon the structure of the old humanity. It is not analogous to the mystery cults, nor to merely one people or one *polis* (although this is the case to the degree that it understands itself as the true Israel), but rather to humanity itself. This is why, in Luke's genealogy of Jesus, the Lord is presented not simply as the son of Abraham and thus the father of a new Israel but also as the son of Adam, which is a claim that resides on a human level (Lk 3:23–38). The Church is the new *cosmopolis*, which consequently, therefore, also truly promises a new *cosmos*, as in Rv 21:1. Its clash with the political *cosmopolis* of Rome is hence of an entirely different kind than the clash between two of the

18. See the presentation of Pauline theology in R. Bultmann, 3rd ed., *Theologie des Neuen Testaments* (Tübingen, 1958), 187–353.

ancient *poleis*. There each would have claimed to embody this *cosmos* and, along with that, the right to rule over it. The Church had no such claim in mind, and it expressly acknowledged that Rome was in fact the *cosmopolis* of this *cosmos*. This was what lay in the background, for example, when early Christians referred to Rome by the cosmic name of Babylon, taken from Gn 11, which was the basic text on the condition of human beings at the time, whereas contemporary Judaism called Rome not Babylon but Edom.[19] But simultaneously this made it clear that it was in the Church that the final and authentic *cosmos* was proclaimed, before which the old *cosmos* would eventually have to give way. The

---

19. On the designation of Rome as Babylon, see 1 Pt 5:13; Rv 14:8, 16:19, 17:5, 18:2.10.21. On the Jewish equation of Rome and Edom, see J. Michl, "Engel," in *Reallexikon für Antike und Christentum* V, 87; K. Hofstetter, "Das Petrusamt in der Kirche des 1. und 2. Jahrhunderts: Jerusalem-Rom," in M. Roesle and O. Cullmann, eds., *Begegnung der Christen* (Festschrift Otto Karrer) (Frankfurt, 1959), 378–79. On the Jewish equation of Rome and Kedar, see K. Schubert, *Die Gemeinde vom Toten Meer* (Munich-Basel, 1958), 83–88.

two-*poleis* doctrine, which from the time of the
Book of Revelation was an enduring component of
the Christian message,[20] was nothing more than
the application of the two-Adams doctrine to the
image of Jerusalem, whose cosmic and eschatological meaning had already been rethought by Paul in
a Christian way in Gal 4:21–31.

The Conflict with Gnosticism

After all that has been said it should be
clear that Christianity confronted the
Greco-Roman world as something revolutionary—
not in the sense of a violent movement to over-
throw the status quo but rather in the sense
of opposing self-assertion through the force of
arms by the stronger power of self-sacrifice, which
conquers through submission, and also in the

---

20. See Ehrhardt, *Politische Metaphysik* II; and for an exposition of the
two-cities image in *The Shepherd of Hermas*, simile 1, see ibid., 52–53. See
also W. Kamlah, *Christentum und Geschichtlichkeit* (Stuttgart, 1951), 159ff.

sense of a profound questioning of the spiritual and intellectual presuppositions that formed the basis of the life of the ancient world and gave shape to its understanding of the *cosmos* and of the order of the universe.[21] Yet the Christian revolution contained its boundaries within itself, and in that respect it differentiated itself from the Gnostic revolution, which was absolutist and which, thanks to Hans Jonas, we know was a radical movement.[22] Inasmuch as it placed itself on the side of the snake and of Cain and Judas, the most despised of all human beings, Gnosticism showed its true colors: It rejected the entire *cosmos*, along with its God, whom it unmasked as a sinister tyrant and jail-keeper; it saw in God and in the religions of the time only the sealing and final shutting of the prison that the *cosmos* was. Its gospel of an alien god was nothing else than a radical form of protest

21. See Ehrhardt, *Politische Metaphysik* II, 19.
22. See H. Jonas, *Gnosis und spätantiker Geist* I-II, 1 (Göttingen, 1954); and also E. Voegelin, *Wissenschaft, Politik und Gnosis* (Munich, 1959).

against everything that up until then had seemed to be holy, good, and upright, and that was now exposed as a prison, which gnosis promised to show the way out of. Here a passionately wild idea, whose urges had long been suppressed, burst upon the scene, and in order to break through like this it seemed that the call of the Christian revolution, sounding from somewhere else entirely, was needed to clear the way beforehand. Hence it is certainly no coincidence that gnosis, which had had a lengthy germination and was now in full flower, immediately attached itself as tightly as it could to Christianity and followed after it for centuries like an evil shadow that could only slowly be shaken off, so that outsiders like Celsus and Plotinus took for granted that Gnosticism and Christianity were one and the same thing.[23] In Christ the revolution-

23. On Celsus, see Origen, *Against Celsus* II, 27; V, 61; VI, 34. On Plotinus, see Porphyry, *The Life of Plotinus* 16. See also Plotinus, *Enneads* II, 9 ("Against the Gnostics"), as well as the interesting marginal comments on *Enneads* II, 9, that are found in various ancient manuscripts.

ary spirituality of Late Antiquity believed that it had finally found the alien God whom, in protest, it could set against the gods of a *cosmos* whose world-order they had increasingly come to understand as a gruesome slavery.[24]

It should not necessarily be surprising that the tone of the Christian revolution could sound like and be confused with that of the Gnostic revolution, although they were fundamentally different from one another. For, as much as Christian belief at the time wished to see the *cosmos* and humanity as transitory and as inadequate and confused and damaged by sin, it never doubted that God's *cosmos* was nonetheless his own and consequently a good work, and that the God of the *cosmos* and the God of Jesus Christ were one and the same God. Christians knew, indeed, that in the end God would replace this world by a better one, which through them had already begun to appear in reality. They also knew,

---

24. See Ehrhardt, *Politische Metaphysik* II, 28.

however, that the present world was not altogether
bad but only stood in need of the transformation
whereby it was supposed to rise to eternal glory. For
this reason it was not difficult for them to see that,
although it was transitory, the world order that they
knew nonetheless possessed a relative goodness
and hence deserved respect within its own framework, and that it was only to be rejected when it
stepped outside this framework and absolutized itself. They found this expressed in the Lord's words,
"Render to Caesar the things that are Caesar's, and
to God the things that are God's" (Mk 12:17). They
found the same teaching in the epistles of the apostles Peter (1 Pt 2:13–17) and Paul (Rom 13:1–7).[25] From
the Old Testament they knew that there was a dis-
tinction between an office and an office-holder. Just
as the king of Babylon could be referred to as God's
servant (Jer 25:9) when he himself neither knew nor

25. On the interpretation of these texts, see ibid., I, 21–28. On the whole
issue, see H. Schlier, *Besinnung auf das Neue Testament* (Freiburg, 1964),
193–211; O. Cullmann, *Der Staat im Neuen Testament* (Tübingen, 1956).

honored this God, so could Rome's imperial powers be deployed at this time to carry out a divine commission, even if these powers were in the hands of highly dubious and unworthy officials. A Christian was obliged to respect God's plan in using them, as long as and insofar as they themselves acted within the framework of the plan that they were assigned to implement. Hence, while the Gnostic revolution was anarchic, inasmuch as it fundamentally questioned every kind of ordinance arising from within the world, the Christian revolution operated within certain boundaries. For, to be sure, it denied the state's traditional understanding of itself and, along with that, its spiritual and intellectual basis, but nonetheless it allowed it a new although essentially restricted validity in its new spiritual and intellectual world.

Consequently the Christian position was much more nuanced than either the Greco-Roman or the Gnostic position. What happened as a result of this as Christians lived through real history? This is the question that will be treated in the following pages, using the examples of a Greek and a Latin theologian, Origen and Augustine. In each case their thinking can only be briefly sketched rather than laid out in its entirety. Before that, however, a rough outline will be proposed of the vision as a whole which, despite minor variations, guided the Fathers, so that at least the coherence of that great spiritual and intellectual current may be evident, apart from which neither Origen nor Augustine are able to be understood properly.[26]

The Fathers' Vision of the Unity of the Peoples

We can begin by observing that for the Fathers the mystery of Christ was, as such, entirely a mystery of unity; we need only recall the great declaration of the Epistle to the Ephesians,

26. For the following remarks I am particularly indebted to the still un-surpassed presentation of H. De Lubac, *Katholizismus als Gemeinschaft* (Einsiedeln, 1963).

where Christ is described as "our peace" and is said
to have broken down the dividing wall and brought
together the different parts of humanity that were
enemies and alienated from one another in order
to form a new man (Eph 2:14–15). This declaration
provided the Fathers with the basic idea for their
understanding of the mystery of Christ. Unity was
not just one among other themes here but rather
the leitmotiv of the whole. This is evident first of
all from the fact that sin appears as a mystery of
division. Thanks to its workings humanity's original unity was shattered into many pieces—that is,
into individuals mutually opposed to each other.
Augustine preserves an especially beautiful variant
on this doctrine from an Eastern tradition when
he mentions in one of his *Expositions of the Psalms*
that the four letters of Adam's name are the same
as the first letters of the four Greek words for the
four points of the compass: "We could think of this
as signifying that the original Adam was scattered
all over the earth. He was at first in a single place;

he fell, and he was somehow fragmented until he filled the earth. But God's mercy collected the shattered pieces, forged them together in the fire of charity, and made what was broken into a single whole once more."[27]

The mystery of Christ, which abolishes sin, was consequently understandable here as a mystery of reunification. But how shall we picture to ourselves this process of unification? The thoughts of the Fathers on this subject can perhaps be sketched broadly as follows: Inasmuch as Christ became a man, something happened to human beingness, to the being of man, in general—that is, to human nature as such. In the view of the Fathers, human-beingness was in fact something unique in all human beings. When we refer to all

27. *Exposition of Psalm* 95, 15, translated by M. Boulding, *The Works of Saint Augustine* III/18 (Hyde Park, N.Y., 2002), 436. See De Lubac, *Katholizismus*, 339–40, for parallel texts from the Early Middle Ages, and also ibid., 31ff, especially 33, note 33, for parallel texts from Alexander of Alexandria and Simeon the New Theologian.

those who have human features as "man," that was
not a mere word for the Fathers; it was so real that
Gregory of Nyssa believed that one could speak
of men in the plural as little as one could speak of
three Gods in the Trinity.[28] And so what happened
in the nature of one human being somehow had
an effect on human nature as a whole and had to
have some bearing on the other possessors of that
nature. If human-beingness was a single living organism, so to speak, then what touched it, wherever
this might have occurred, touched humanity in its
totality. When God became a man, then, and drew
a particular man to himself and thus into union
with God, he thereby touched the human-beingness
of all men, and with that this entire organism was
moved towards God. The human-beingness of Jesus
Christ was, as it were, the divine fishing rod that
caught the human-beingness of all men and was
now pulling it in, so that all the human-beingness of

28. See *On the Making of Man* 16; *Against Eunomius* III (PG 45, 592). See
De Lubac, *Katholizismus*, 26–27, 333–37.

all men would be brought into the unity of the body of Christ, the God-man, and out of the fatal division that characterized the isolation known as sin.

This mystery of being drawn in is portrayed in ever-new images. Human nature is the lost sheep of the gospel, which the Good Shepherd brings back to the sheepfold;[29] it is the living coin that bears the image of God and hence is to be given back to God, just as the coins that bear the emperor's likeness are to be given back to him.[30] Christ, on the other hand, is the needle that pierces painfully in his Passion but that in the end rejoins everything, thus restoring the robe that Adam had torn apart by sewing together the two peoples, Jews and gentiles, making them forever one.[31] Briefly said, the being of Jesus Christ and the

29. Numerous examples are cited in De Lubac, *Katholizismus*, 23; see esp. Gregory of Nyssa, *On the Song of Songs* 2 (PG 44, 801). See also F. Malmberg, *Ein Leib–ein Geist* (Freiburg, 1960), 223–43, esp. 238.
30. See, e.g., Augustine, *Exposition of Psalm* 94, 2.
31. See Paschasius Radbertus, *Commentary on Matthew* 9 (PL 120, 666); De Lubac, *Katholizismus*, 33.

message of Jesus Christ introduced a new dynamic into humanity, the dynamic of the passage out of a being that was divided into many individual parts and into the unity of Jesus Christ, the unity of God. And the Church was, so to speak, nothing other than this dynamic, namely, humanity's movement towards the unity of God. The Church was, in keeping with its very essence, a passage from a human-beingness that was torn apart and adversarial to a new human-beingness marked by the reunification of its shattered fragments.

This was precisely what the Fathers wanted to express when they referred to the Church as the body of Christ. And in fact they meant still more, something much more concrete, when they used this term. For this phrase—into which streamed as early as the Epistle to the Ephesians the whole breadth of hope in the fulfillment of the unity of the universe under the name of Christ and in his reality—had an utterly concrete meaning from the time of the First Epistle to the Corinthians: "The cup of blessing which we bless, is it not a participation in the blood of Christ? The bread which we break, is it not a participation in the body of Christ? Because there is one bread, we who are many are one body, for we all partake of the one bread" (1 Cor 10:16–17). This was the very first text in which Paul used the term "body of Christ," and it remained the basic one for the Fathers. Its use by the Fathers pointed to the utterly concrete *Sitz im Leben* of all the profound thoughts of theirs, and of their successors, that eventually lent themselves to this theme over the course of time. The unheard-of new thing toward which history aimed was the drawing in of humankind into the unity of God, which began in the life and suffering of the Lord. The unfolding of this beginning into the concrete history of individual human beings occurred, then, in the celebration of the Eucharist that was built on the foundation of Baptism. Here, at the Lord's table, what happened was that human beings, in eating Christ's body, themselves became Christ's body and were assimilated into the body of the New Adam. Here, at God's table, was the place where at the same time there was true communication of human beings with one another: the place where human beings communicated with God and simultaneously communicated among themselves was where they came together to form the new man.

Thus everything was placed on a completely concrete basis, beyond the realm of speculation. But this was not sufficient to satisfy the Fathers: they transgressed the limits of the cultic; or, rather, they brought the cultic into the everyday. The undifferentiated sharing in table fellowship of all believers only made sense in their view if believers really overcame their differences as well and lived as brothers. The brotherhood of Christians, and indeed the brotherly feelings of Christians towards all human beings, was the necessary consequence of that intra-human communication that was indissolubly bound up with the sacrament of the Lord's Supper. Hence "communion" was likewise

an appeal to individuals to come out of themselves
and out of their individualism, to lose themselves
in order truly to find themselves in the larger
whole (Mt 10:39). The passage that is identified
with the Church was realized in individuals as a
passage from the primacy of the individual ego
to the unity of the members of the body of Christ.
The Easter law of the Pasch, or passage, was in fact
the basic law of Christianity, which, built on the
foundation of the Easter sacrament from which
the Church took its life, was written once for all.
The Fathers' vision of the unity of humanity began
to take on very defined outlines here: in the net
of eucharistic communities which the Christian
mission cast across the whole *oikumene*, that communication of human beings with one another and
with God, which was the final goal of the Christian
experience, had already begun. For that eucharistic
community was brotherhood, woven together in
the one single brotherliness of all God's tables in
this world, and those table-communities, again,

were fundamentally open; they were not closed circles but stood rather as an invitation on the part of God—one that had a particular form and shape—to all people to participate in God's eternal wedding banquet. The Church's eucharistic net was, so to speak, the concrete shape of the net that God lowered into the sea of this world in order to catch humanity for himself and lead it to the shore of eternity.[32]

32. See J. Ratzinger, *Volk und Haus Gottes in Augustins Lehre von der Kirche* (Munich, 1954); idem, *Das neue Volk Gottes* (Düsseldorf, 1969), 77–89; Y. Congar, "De la communion des Eglises à une ecclésiologie de l'Eglise universelle," in Y. Congar and B. D. Dupuy, *L'épiscopat et l'Eglise universelle* (Paris, 1962), 227–60.

2

THE
CHRISTIAN
GNOSIS OF
ORIGEN

The Meaning of National Identity in Origen

The Negative Aspect

The problem of how to balance human values with those of national identity was one of the major issues in the debate between the Hellenist Celsus and the Christian Origen. Celsus not only accused Christians of forming an illegal conspiracy;[1] he also asserted that they were persons without a fatherland who had no allegiance anywhere, and that they had betrayed their nation's laws and in so doing had placed themselves outside all law. "I would like to ask them where they come from and who the author of their fatherland's laws is. They cannot produce him. They are from there [i.e., Judaism] and they have their teacher and leader from nowhere else. They are fallen-away Jews."[2] Inasmuch as Christians have

1. See Origen, *Against Celsus* I, 1.
2. Ibid., V, 33.

abandoned their fatherland's laws and disregard-
ed the value of national identity, they have placed
themselves outside the divine ordering of the
world, in which the insertion of an individual human being within the framework of a particular
nation and its political and religious structures
was something essential. For God did not govern
the earth by himself in direct fashion but from the
very beginning had portioned it out to different
overseers, who had given the individual peoples
their religious and political laws. Religion, consequently, was part of national identity, and the fact
that a person belonged to a particular nation was
something that was decreed by divine governance.[3]
With his doctrine of an apportioning of the world
to different regents, Celsus set out a schema that

3. See ibid., V, 25–26. On the origin of the schema of a divine monarch
who rules not by himself but through satraps, see E. Peterson, "Der
Monotheismus als politisches Problem," in *Theologische Traktate*
(Munich, 1951), 50ff, 72–73, esp. 130–31, with note 15; E. Peterson, "Das
Problem des Nationalismus im alten Christentum," in idem., *Früh-
kirche, Judentum and Gnosis* (Freiburg, 1959), 56–57.

not only had made deep inroads into the Greco-Roman world but also had found a welcome, in the doctrine of the angels of the peoples, in the thinking of Late Judaism,[4] for which the Greek translation of Dt 32:8 provided the inspiration: "When the Most High divided the peoples, when he scattered the sons of Adam, he set out boundaries for the nations, corresponding to the number of the angels of God." This verse was also the point of departure for the dialogue between Origen and Celsus on the value and limits of national identity.

Origen accepted the fact that the world was portioned out to different heavenly rulers, but he added that there was still a question as to who planned this apportionment and how it happened. The

4. See Michl, V, 75.87; J. Daniélou, *Théologie du Judéo-Christianisme* (Tournai, 1958), 142–43; idem, "Les sources juives de la doctrine des anges des nations chez Origène," *Recherches des Sciences Religieuses* 38 (1951): 132–37; idem, *Origène* (Paris, 1948), 222–35; E. Peterson, "Das Problem des Nationalismus," 51-63, note 35. The enduring significance of these ideas has been explored in depth in M. Buber, *An der Wende: Reden über das Judentum* (Cologne, 1952), 13–33.

answer to this he took from the story of the Tower of Babel in Gn 11:1–9. Understood in a spiritual way, this account implied that humanity had maintained a single language as long as it possessed a single mind. Seen from a spiritual perspective, it had remained in the East as long as it kept itself in the spirit of light and its eternal radiance. When it moved away from this spiritual East it descended to the plain of Shinar, which in Hebrew means "loss of teeth"—that is, the loss of the tools for nourishment and of the ability to take in the spiritual food that had served as the foundation of life on which it had previously subsisted. "When they gather material things, then, and join to heaven things that cannot be joined to it in order to build a way to what is immaterial with material objects, then they say, 'Come, let us make bricks and bake them in the fire' (Gn 11:3)."[5] As a result of this attempt it now happened that they were given over to angels of a more or less harsh disposition to whom they were

5. *Against Celsus* V, 30.

intended to be subject until they did penance for their misdeed. These angels were the ones who gave languages to the individual peoples and led them away to different parts of the earth, whether to fertile or infertile lands, each according to the degree of its guilt.[6] There was only *one* people, spiritually understood, that remained in the East. That was Israel, which was therefore not subjected to any angelic power; instead, it continued on as the portion of the Lord God himself.[7] Origen realized from the outset that the problem of national identity had nothing to do with Israel; it was never a nation in any real sense but rather the only part of humanity that had not fallen into the prison of national identity but instead had remained what all others

6. See ibid., V, 31. On the issue of language, see Peterson, "Das Problem des Nationalismus," 61–62, note 35.

7. See *Against Celsus*, V, 31. On the two traditions concerning Israel (according to one, Israel was not subject to an angel but directly to the Lord, and according to another, it had Michael or, following some texts, Michael and Gabriel as guardian angels), see Michl, V, 75.87; Daniélou, *Théologie du Judéo-Christianisme*, 143, note 36.

could and should have been—namely, humanity in a direct relationship with God. For that reason Origen rejected the praise that Celsus bestowed on the Jews because, in contrast to the Christians, Celsus claimed, they followed a national religion and kept within the realm of the God-given order of the peoples.[8] But, on the other hand, he also had to defend the Jews against the reproach that their awareness of having been chosen made them arrogant and foolish, since, as Celsus claimed once again, other people had identical or similar laws and worshiped the same High God, albeit under different names.[9] On the contrary, Origen replied, Israel gave the world the holy symbols of the city of God, of the Temple, and of its impressive form of worship, and along with that it hinted that there was something above and beyond the nations that was primordial, original, and common to all.[10] In particular, Israel gave human beings that true state which Plato

8. See *Against Celsus* V, 25–26.   9. See ibid., V, 41–59.
10. See ibid., V, 45–46.

could only dream of without having been able to conceive of it in all its clarity.[11]

In seeing Israel's merit in the fact that it did not put itself under the rubric of national identity but instead remained "humanity" pure and simple, and that in so doing it formed the true state which was the only true home for all human beings, Origen also sketched out clearly his understanding of the Church and of its relationship to the national order. Before considering this, though, it will be worthwhile to explore his concept of the nation more closely. It is obvious to us that the angels of the peoples point to a national identity. They were the ones that allotted to the individual peoples their language and their land, which are the constitutive elements of a nation, and it is to them that national cultures owed their existence.[12] From

11. See ibid., V, 43.
12. On language and land, see ibid., V, 30; on the founding of national cultures, see Origen, *On First Principles* III, 2. See also Peterson, "Das Problem des Nationalismus," 55–56, note 35.

what has been said it should also be obvious that
Origen saw in these angels an instance of the punishment that was a consequence of the falling
away of the peoples from the spiritual unity of humankind. He believed, moreover, that the angels
of the peoples were usurpers who lawlessly seized
power for themselves and sought out territories
that they could dominate, which corresponded to
the godlessness of human beings that had opened
the door to their seizure of power. But humanity's only righteous ruler was Jesus Christ.[13] The
archons, as Origen refers to the angels of the peoples, using a Greek word that means "rulers" or
"princes" and that often had a sinister spiritual
connotation in early Christian literature, were
powers of disorder and not of order, their justice
was injustice and their laws were unlawful.[14] That
is why, when he tempted Jesus, Satan could point
to the kingdoms of this world as to his own royal

13. See *Against Celsus* VIII, 33.
14. See ibid., V, 32.

territory, because their archons were actually the devil's lackeys.[15]

In his vivid explanation of the parable in Lk 12:58, Origen elaborated on this understanding of the archons. The parable says that the man who is going with his accuser to the magistrate must make an effort to free himself of his accuser wherever possible while he is on the way, so as not to be handed over to the judge and be imprisoned. The accuser was, according to Origen, a symbol of the bad angel who was placed alongside every human being and who saw his ultimate objective as dragging that person to the magistrate, who in turn symbolized one of the archons. As soon as he arrived there, he was subject to judgment and condemnation. The person who at the conclusion of his life fell into the hands of an archon had thus failed to arrive at his final goal, and he ended up before his bad angel's master. Now this archon,

15. See Mt 4:8–9; Lk 4:5–7; Origen, *Fragment* 66 on Mt 4:8 (GCS Origenes XII/1, 42).

whom the bad angels of each individual human being served, was the angel of the people for that individual. The bad angels were the army that the angel of the people had at his command; they belonged to him, and with their help he oppressed the people that he had been allotted and made them submissive.[16] This also meant, then, that whoever submitted himself to a national identity and, instead of thinking and living along human lines, thought and lived within the confines of national identity, thereby submitted himself to his bad angel. Whoever put himself in the category of a national identity had thereby betaken himself to

16. See Origen, *Homily on Luke* 35. I cannot accept Peterson's explanation in "Das Problem des Nationalismus," 56, note 35, when he says that the two-angels doctrine was carried over to the angels of the peoples and adds, "But this ultimately means that the angels of the peoples can be viewed both under the aspect of the spirit of the people and under that of the soul of the people." In fact the two-angels doctrine (incidentally with an express appeal in the *Homily on Luke* 35, 3 to *The Shepherd of Hermas*) is used only in reference to individual human beings; the figure of the angel of the people—i.e., the archon—remains unambiguous and clear: he is the ruler of the relevant bad angel.

prison and handed himself over to the archon and to the dominating power of evil.

It is clear from the following passage that this is no present-day modernizing reinterpretation of Origen but rather his authentic meaning: "Each of us has his own bad angel near him, who clings to him and whose task it is to bring us to the archon and say, 'O archon (for example, the one for the kingdom of the Persians), I have brought into your custody this man, who lived in your dominion, as was necessary. The other archons could not draw him over to themselves, not even the one [i.e., Christ] who boasted that he had come in order to carry off men from all regions, from the Persians and the Greeks and from every nation, and bring them into the kingdom of God.' For Christ our Lord has conquered all the archons and brought the peoples everywhere throughout their domains out of the captivity of the archons and led them to himself for salvation's sake. You too used to be under an archon's rule. Jesus has come and has snatched you from the wicked power and brought you over to God the Father. But our bad angel is accompanying us and is trying to lead us to our archon."[17] According to this text (whose main points were anticipated in the Epistles to the Ephesians and Colossians),[18] the salvific work of Jesus consisted precisely in the fact that he conquered the archons and led human beings out of the prison of national identity into the unity of God and into the unity of a common humanity.

In a difficult passage in his work *On First Principles* Origen tried to deepen his understanding of these predominantly salvation-history sayings in a metaphysical way, and here he confronted the problem of how to interpret the prophetic texts of the Old Testament. In so doing he arrived, first, at the insight that the sayings about Jerusalem only made sense when they were referred not simply to

17. *Homily on Luke* 35, 6–7. The translator thanks Joseph Lienhard, SJ, for shedding light on a difficult phrase.
18. See H. Schlier, *Mächte und Gewalten im Neuen Testament* (Freiburg, 1958).

the historical this-worldly Jerusalem but to Jerusalem as a spiritual entity, to the heavenly Jerusalem. This insight yielded a further one—namely, that all the other seemingly political prophecies, which were so abundant in the Old Testament, ultimately had nothing to do in fact with the political structures of Babylon and Egypt and Tyre and so forth, but rather with the spiritual entities that each of them symbolized. Just as there was a Jerusalem in heaven, so there were other places there as well, higher and lower, better and worse. The prophecies concerning individual peoples had to do with these otherworldly places that corresponded to earthly nations. Just as there were Israelites in the hereafter, for example, so there were Egyptians there, and Tyrians and Babylonians, and so forth. In other words, there were, according to Origen's controversial understanding, different spiritual rankings corresponding to the different degrees of falling away from an original and primordial beatific state. Whether a person was born in Egypt or Edom or Babylon in the present world, then, depended on the spiritual decision that he previously made in the other world, to the degree that his spirit culpably departed from the ranking that had been accorded to it. But that meant that nations were not accidental constructs but rather metaphysical entities. They pointed to a particular stage of falling away from the divine world-intellect.[19] Hence Origen employed a comprehensive theology or, better said, a theological metaphysics of the nation. But the nation seen in its metaphysical depth

19. See *On First Principles* IV, 3, 8–15. See also *Commentary on Matthew XIV*, 13 (on Mt 18:23–35): "Just as 'the Jerusalem that is above' is the mother (Gal 4:26) of Paul and of those like him, so there may be a mother of others after the analogy of Jerusalem—the mother, for example, of Syene in Egypt, or Sidon, or of as many cities as are named in the Scriptures. Then, just as Jerusalem is 'a bride adorned for her husband' (Rv 21:2), Christ, so there may be mothers of certain powers who have been allotted to them as wives or brides. And just as there are certain children of Jerusalem as mother and of Christ as father, so there would be certain children of Syene or Memphis or Tyre or Sidon and of the archons set over them." Translated by J. Patrick in *Ante-Nicene Fathers* IV (Grand Rapids, Mich., 1986), 466–67, alt.

was not a vehicle of salvation; it was, instead, part of the order of the falling away and therefore, in the last resort, constitutive of disorder.[20]

After this, in his treatise *On First Principles*, Origen discussed Israel's mission. The seventy men who, according to Ex 1:1–5, left Israel for Egypt signified Israel in its totality—in other words, Israel as a spiritual entity. The spirits that clung to the vision of God and descended into Egypt, which symbolized this world, did so in order, like the stars of heaven, to cast light on men and lead them on the return journey. Israel's mission, which was fulfilled in the Church, was thus the leading of humankind

---

20. See *Against Celsus* V, 32: "We would not agree with Celsus's opinion when he maintains that because of the overseers that have been allotted to the parts of the earth 'the practices done by each nation are right.' Moreover, we do not want to do their practices 'in the way that pleases them.' For we see that it is pious to break 'customs which have existed in each locality from the beginning' and to adopt better and more divine laws given us by Jesus, as the most powerful being, 'delivering us from this present evil world' (Gal 1:4) and from 'the rulers of this world who are coming to nought' (1 Cor 2:6)." Translated by H. Chadwick in *Origen: Contra Celsum* (Cambridge, 1980), 289.

on its journey homeward from out of the order of the archons, out of the order of national identity, into the one order of God, which encompassed all peoples and languages.[21]

Positive Statements

I have come across only one passage in Origen that seems to express another and more positive evaluation of national identity. It

21. See *On First Principles* IV, 3, 11–12. In his *Théologie du Judéo-Christianisme*, 143, note 36, as well as in *Das Geheimnis der Geschichte* (Stuttgart, 1955), 63, J. Daniélou relates this interpretation of the descent of the seventy into Egypt to the doctrine of the angels of the peoples. He sees here a connection with the Hebrew version of Dt 32:8, circulated by Symmachus, whch refers to the division of the peoples "according to the number of the sons of Israel," instead of "according to the number of the angels of God" in the Septuagint version. In his view both readings combine to make possible an allegorical identification of the seventy souls of Ex 1:5 and the seventy angels of the peoples of Dt 32:8, which appears here in Origen. Although I certainly see the possibility of such a linkage, it does not seem to me to be sufficiently evident with respect to the passage in question. I am not convinced that the seventy men have any direct relationship to the angels of the peoples; they only witness to Israel's heavenly origin and its mission in the world.

appears in connection with Jn 4:38: "I sent you to reap that for which you did not labor. Others have labored, and you have entered into their labor." According to Origen, the first understanding of the "others" into whose labor the apostles entered is Moses and the prophets. But, as the result of extended reflection makes clear, they can also be understood as the angels of the peoples who have striven for their portion and brought it under their control. In the wake of Christ's salvific work, men "are taken captive for the service of Jesus Christ (2 Cor 10:5) from the portion of all [the angels of the peoples], through the gospel service of the apostles, evangelists, and teachers. They are being led so that the peoples may become the one inheritance of Jesus Christ."[22] Origen continues by de-

---

22. *Commentary on John* XIII, 49. The translation is imperfect insofar as the contrast between the portion of the angels of the peoples and the inheritance of Christ is not as strong as it is in the original Greek, which makes clear that the assignment of a portion to an angel is as essential as is the ordering of Christ to the whole.

claring that Jn 4:36, which says that the sower and
the reaper should rejoice together, does not contra-
dict this interpretation, so long as the angels of the
peoples are taken to be good angels.[23] Then, in fact,
their returning to stand before Christ, who leads
the way home to God's harvest, is what they have
been preparing for, and the joy that they share with
the harvesters, the apostles, makes good sense.
The work of the apostles would then signify the
eschatological completion of the service carried out
by the angels of the peoples. But Origen expressly
treats all of this—which, relative to his other interpretations, provides a much more positive evaluation of national identity—merely as a nonbinding
hypothesis that he simply offers as a possibility for
consideration.[24]

---

23. See ibid.
24. See ibid. See also the beginning of Origen's exposition, which is
outspoken in its stance of questioning. In addition, a little later Her-
acleon's exegesis is worked out by Origen in a different way, and the
choice of the two interpretations is left up to the reader.

The positive meaning that he allows to be drawn from this attempted interpretation seems to me, again, to be evident in *On First Principles* when, in commenting on 1 Cor 2:6–8, he introduces his teaching on the three kinds of wisdom—namely, God's, the world's, and that of the princes of this world.[25] God's wisdom has made its appearance in Christ. The world's wisdom is the knowledge that knows nothing of God and nothing of the meaning of the world or of higher things in general; it is simply worldly knowledge of such things as poetry, grammar, rhetoric, geometry, music, and perhaps medicine as well. The wisdom of the princes of this world, finally, is something that we meet in the secret philosophy of the Egyptians, in the astrology of the Chaldeans, and in Indian and Greek speculation about the highest being. These philosophies, which are linked to their respective peoples and which lead eventually to the divine foundations of

25. See *On First Principles* III, 3, 1–3.

the world (in contrast to the previously mentioned forms of knowledge that deal with merely human things), are in Origen's view not the work of human intelligence but have been taught by the angels of the peoples, the princes of this world, to their respective peoples. It is a matter, then, of a typically national wisdom having to do with a particular people. Hence it is easy to understand why these world-princes conspired against the supernational wisdom of God in Jesus Christ, of whose coming into the world in order to destroy their wisdom they had heard: "The kings of the earth set themselves, and the rulers take counsel together, against the Lord and his anointed" (Ps 2:2). This is the conspiracy that decided on the Lord's death and arranged for it without in fact knowing who it was that they were dealing with, "for if they had known, they would not have crucified the Lord of glory" (1 Cor 2:8). Origen infers from Saint Paul's words that the archons were in no way intentionally leading the peoples astray but were simply passing on to them their own knowledge.[26] Perhaps this thesis can be seen in tandem with the afore-mentioned passages from the *Commentary on John* in such a way that, as viewed from Origen's perspective, the place of the angels of the peoples—in other words, the place occupied by national identity as a separate and surpassingly important mental construct—was simply not the same after Christ as it was before Christ. Before Christ a certain good faith could still be conceded to the angels of the peoples, and national identity was still in a state of relative innocence; it still possessed its genuine preparatory function. After Christ, on the other hand, it could only continue to exist in the form of the truth-resistant self-assertion of a superannuated order. That national identity after Christ had no genuine legitimacy was something that Origen declared quite frequently and clearly; that it had once had a genuine preparatory function does not ap-

26. See ibid., III, 3, 3.

pear with equal clarity in his writings, although in light of what has been said it seems to correspond to his original intention.

The Place of the Church

The Eschatological Revolution

For Christians, in Origen's understanding, the fatherland was replaced by the Church, in which he saw "the fatherland according to God," "a new form of fatherland, based on God's Word."[27] Origen agreed with Celsus that the Christian faith in fact constituted a shattering of the ancient principle of binding together religion, on the one hand, and national and political identity, on the other. Christians had abandoned the old bonds and joined the holy pilgrimage of the peoples to Mount Zion that was referred to in Is 2:2–4. Their leader was Christ, whom as the new people they followed. This people turned swords into plow-

27. *Against Celsus* VIII, 75.

shares and spears into pruning hooks; it no longer took up weapons against any other people and no longer learned the ways of war, for its members had become "sons of peace" in Jesus, "who leads us now, instead of the fatherland's ordinances, in which we once lived when we were alienated from God's covenant (Eph 2:12)."[28] For Christians the law of Christ had replaced the absolute rule of national laws, and it had revealed that the old laws were valueless. It was true that Christ, "our chorus-master and our teacher," came from the Jews, but with his word he acquired the whole *oikumene* as his portion.[29] God's law, which through Jesus Christ was valid for the whole *oikumene,* had replaced the national ordinances in all their narrowness. The expression of this new worldwide order was the one Church that encompassed all peoples. It was for this reason that Christians accepted no political offices and refused military service: they had their

28. Ibid., V, 33.
29. See ibid., V, 36.

own *polis* with their own offices, whose service was more divine and more imperative than that of earthly states.[30] It was for this reason as well that Christians considered it legitimate to bypass the laws of the state for the sake of the better and truer laws of Jesus Christ.[31] Indeed, Origen did not hesitate in his own way to acknowledge the correctness of Celsus's accusation that Christians had entered into an unlawful conspiracy when he said, "Suppose that a man were living among the Scythians whose laws are contrary to the divine law, who had no opportunity to go elsewhere and was compelled to live among them; such a man for the sake of the true law, though illegal among the Scythians, would rightly form associations with like-minded people contrary to the law of the Scythians. So, at the bar of truth, the laws of the nations such as those about images and godless

30. See ibid., VIII, 74–75.
31. See ibid., V, 27–28, 32, 35–40.

polytheism are laws of the Scythians or, if possible, more impious than theirs. Therefore it is not wrong to form associations against the laws for the sake of truth. For, just as it would be right for people to form associations secretly to kill a tyrant who had seized control of their city, so too, since the devil, as Christians call him, and falsehood reign as tyrants, Christians form associations against the devil contrary to his laws, in order to save others whom they might be able to persuade to abandon the law which is like that of the Scythians and of a tyrant."[32]

The Limits of the Christian Revolution

The kind of Christianity that revolutionizes the world and is not in the least concerned to hide or lie about its revolutionary character is marked by an eschatological radicalness. There is no doubt that the radicalness of Origen's

32. Ibid. I, 1 (Chadwick, *Origen*, 7, alt.).

revolutionary ethos, with its fundamental rejection
of natural ordinances, bordered on Gnosticism.
Yet even in his theology of humanity and of the
peoples he remained a member of the Christian
Church. In other words, the revolution that he proclaimed was not a mere denial of the *cosmos* and
of the way that the world was structured, but in
the last resort a true affirmation of it. That is clear
in the programmatic rejection of a god who was,
in Gnostic terminology, "new" or "unknown." The
God of the Christians, on the contrary, as Origen
explained, was not a new God, even though his
appearance in human form had happened only recently. He was in fact "the firstborn of all creation"
(Col 1:15); he was the very one to whom, at the creation of man, God spoke the words, "Let us make
man in our image and likeness" (Gn 1:26).[33] In so

---

33. See ibid., V, 37: "This is no reason why we should say that a new
god, that was not formerly a god and was not even know to men, really
exists. However, even if the Son of God, 'the firstborn of all creation'
(Col 1:15), seems to have become man recently, yet he is not in fact new

doing Origen abolished the typical Gnostic division between the God of creation, the "old" God, and the God of salvation, the "new," "unknown," God; *cosmos* and Christ, creation and covenant were all bound together. Faith in Christ, to be sure, revolutionized the present form of the world, but it was not opposed to the *cosmos* as such; rather, it disclosed its true meaning for the first time.

This becomes clearer in the actual formation and description of the Christian revolution. Origen drew attention to the fact that there were two laws—the law of nature, which originated with God, and the written law of individual states. When the two were in conflict, it was obvious that the law of nature had priority.[34] For the sake of a better knowledge of that law it had always been the

---

on that account. For the divine scriptures know that he is the oldest of all created beings, and that it was to him that God said of the creation of man, 'Let us make man in our image and likeness'" (Chadwick, *Origen*, 294).

34. See ibid.

duty of philosophers even to deny the fatherland's
laws when necessary and to pursue the philosophical insight provided by the law of nature.[35] Christians who followed the one express law of God even
against the directives of the political power only
did something that, at bottom, philosophy had
long recognized as right. This was how the Chris-

35. See ibid., V, 35: "For if, on account of their philosophy and the in-
structions which they have received against superstition, they [i.e.,
pagan philosophers] should eat, in disregard of their native laws, what
was interdicted by their fathers, why should the Christians (since the
gospel requires them not to busy themselves about statues and images,
or even about any of the created works of God but to ascend on high
and present the soul to the Creator), when acting in a similar manner
to the philosophers, be censured for so doing?" Translated by F. Crom-
bie in *Ante-Nicene Fathers* IV (Grand Rapids, Mich., 1986), 277. Origen's
emphasis on the similar behavior of philosophers and Christians is
especially helpful in evaluating his Christian-revolutionary stance.
Note the sentence later in the same chapter where Origen says that a
philosopher who maintained his fatherland's customs when they were
unreasonable would not be acting philosophically. See also ibid., V,
26–37. Particularly significant is ibid., V, 28, where Origen shows that
linking religion to a people's identity would have a relativizing effect
on the latter.

tian revolution came to be linked to the philosophical opposition, which embodied the reaction of the values of nature against the authoritarian and arbitrary cast of the political powers.[36] Although the Christian revolution appeared as nothing more at first than an attack on the *cosmos* as such, it ultimately (as was the case with the opposition of the philosophers) even turned out to be useful to it. Origen was completely unhesitant in that regard in the very passages in his writings where he was most severe in his rejection of the existing system. When he explained that, for the sake of their new *polis*, the Church, Christians were unprepared to take on any political or military offices, he was saying at the same time that it was part of the essence of the Church to contribute to the salvation not only of all those who were within the Church but also of all those who were outside it.[37] Christians,

36. On the philosophical opposition, see Ehrhardt, *Politische Metaphysik* I, 247ff, 308–9; II, 1–2, 34–35.

37. See *Against Celsus* VIII, 75: "If Christians do avoid these responsi-

in fact, were even greater benefactors of the fatherland than other citizens inasmuch as they contributed to the education of the human race and taught devotion to the God of all states. Even when they did not participate in any conventional way in military service, they nonetheless served the king in a much more effective way by praying for those who went off to war in a just cause, and by their prayers they conquered the demons (Origen may have meant the angels of the peoples) that were responsible for wars and that disturbed the peace.[38]

---

bilities, it is not with the motive of shirking the public services of life. But they keep themselves for a more divine and necessary service in the Church of God for the sake of the salvation of men. Here it is necessary and right for them to be leaders and to be concerned about all men, both those who are within the Church, that they may live better every day, and those who appear to be outside it, that they may become familiar with the sacred words and acts of worship . . . and so be united to the supreme God through the Son of God" (Chadwick, *Origen*, 510).

38. See ibid., VIII, 73–74, esp. 73: "We who by our prayers destroy all demons which stir up wars, violate oaths, and disturb the peace, are of more help to the emperors than those who seem to be doing the fighting" (Chadwick, *Origen*, 509).

Here too Origen stayed true to himself by teaching that it was not only the nation and its territory that should be prayed for but also righteousness, in opposition to the demonic self-will that destroyed peace. At the same time, however, he showed that this revolutionary stance with respect to ancient (and, for that matter, contemporary) nationalism did not obstruct real patriotism—namely, a sense of responsibility for the true well-being of the fatherland—but rather actually opened the way towards it. He compared Christians with the pagan priests who likewise did not participate in military service because of the higher task that engaged them, which was to elicit the mercy of the gods. Christians, by contrast, were humanity's true priests who, far from being their enemies, through serving God also simultaneously and in the highest sense served their fellow human beings and the world itself in its totality.[39] When,

39. See ibid., VIII, 73.

finally, Origen explained that teaching devotion
to God had passed over from the Jews to the
Christians, who had adapted their laws to the
conditions of their respective states,[40] this showed
that, for Origen, despite his revolt against the
lofty claims that accompanied national identity
and that were symbolized by the angels of the peoples, even in the Christian era the various struc-
tural differences among the peoples could have a
certain right of domicile in the Church. What he
fought against was clearly only the subordination
of the holy to political and national identity. But
once the absolute freedom and priority of the holy
was clarified, the characteristics of the different
peoples could reappear in their own place and in
their own order.

40. See ibid., IV, 22.

Summary

When we look back on what has been said, it is clear that for Origen Christianity still existed primarily as a revolutionary breakthrough and as a release from the prison of a dying world. The outlines of the new order, however, remained unclear and murky. This new order, towards which Origen was looking, was at bottom not a renewal of something this-worldly but rather the eschatological kingdom of peace in which the Babylonian division of humanity was overcome, the rule of the angels of the peoples was abolished, and the entire *oikumene* was brought together into the one *polis* of Jesus Christ. Origen's fundamental affirmation of nature and of the *cosmos* mitigated his eschatological radicalness to the degree that tentatives towards the establishment of peace between the Church and the world before the arrival of the *eschaton* appear clearly in his writings, although he himself saw no opportunity for thinking such a thing through. And, indeed, no one will be able to dispute that Christianity as Origen understood it can only with difficulty be thought of in association with conservatism, and never with legalism, but rather it bears a revolutionary force that is ready to call for a conspiracy against everything "Scythian" whenever and wherever it appears.

3

AUGUSTINE'S DEBATE WITH ROME'S POLITICAL THEOLOGY

The Rejection of Rome's Political Theology

As in the case of Origen, Augustine's point of departure for a political theology was polemical. The fall of Rome in 410 had, once again, elicited a pagan reaction. "Where were the graves of the apostles?" was the outcry. They had obviously been unable to protect Rome, the city that was unconquered the entire time that it had entrusted itself to the protection of its local gods. Rome's defeat was conspicuous proof that the Creator God whom Christian faith revered had no interest in political happenings. This God might well be concerned with man's eternal happiness, but events had demonstrated—even vividly—that he was unconcerned with the political realm. The domain of politics clearly had its own set of laws, which had no bearing on the supreme God; hence it should have its own religion as well.[1]

1. See Augustine, *The City of God* I–V, which deals at great length with what is only briefly sketched out here.

What the masses demanded more out of a general feeling, that in addition to the main religion there also had to be a religion for this-worldly and especially for political things, could be given a much deeper underpinning based on Antiquity's philosophical convictions. One need only recall the Platonic axiom formulated by Apuleius: "Between God and man there is no contact."[2] Platonism was utterly convinced of the infinite gulf between God and the world, spirit and matter. God's direct dealing with the things of the world would necessarily have appeared to it as completely impossible. God's responsibility for the world was met by intermediate beings to which a person would have to have recourse when it was a matter of the things of this world.[3] In this exaggerated concept of God's transcendence, according to which he was removed from the world and cut off from the concrete activities associated with human life, Augustine rightly observed the

2. *On the God of Socrates* 4, cited in *The City of God* IX, 16.
3. See *The City of God* VIII–IX.

seed of a revolt against the all-embracing claims of Christian faith, which could never tolerate the exclusion of the political from the providence of the one God. In the face of the pagan reaction, which aimed at reinstituting the religious status of the this-worldly *polis* and, along with that, relegating the Christian religion (which looked forward to the next world) to the private sphere, Augustine began by making two fundamental assertions.

The Untruthfulness of the Political Religion

His first assertion was that the political religion of Rome had no truth in it. It was built upon the canonization of custom as opposed to truth.[4] This rejection of the truth, or rather this

4. See ibid., IV, 31, where Augustine says of the Roman polymath Varro: "It might seem that I am guessing here, except for the fact that Varro himself states quite openly in another place, where he is speaking of religious rites, that there are many things that are true which it is not useful for the common people to know, and many also which, even if false, it is expedient for the populace to think true. . . . The malignant demons take great delight in this deception, for it means that they have

stand against the truth for the sake of custom, was
frequently espoused by the representatives of Roman religion themselves—Scaevola, Varro, Seneca.[5]
What was contrary to the truth was acceptable for

both the deceivers and the deceived in their possession" (translated by
W. Babcock, *The Works of Saint Augustine* I/6 and I/7 [Hyde Park, N.Y.,
2012–13], I,139). Shortly before, at IV, 30, he had said of the Spanish Stoic philosopher Quintus Lucilius Balbus: "As anyone can see, he is trying
hard, out of respect for the city's established customs, to praise the
religion of his ancestors and wants desperately to separate it out from
superstition, but he can find no way to do this" (Babcock, *Augustine* I,
138). At VI, 4 he speaks again of Varro: "He has admitted that, when he
wrote his books on divine matters, he was not writing about the truth
that belongs to nature but about the falsehood that belongs to error. As
I mentioned in the fourth book [of *The City of God*], he has stated this
more clearly elsewhere. For he said that, if he were himself founding
a new city, he would have written in accord with the rule of nature,
but since he found himself situated in an already-established city, he
could do nothing but follow its customs" (Babcock, *Augustine* I, 190).
One cannot help but recall Tertullian's magnificent statement in *On the
Veiling of Virgins* 1 that Christ referred to himself not as the custom but
as the truth. See J. N. Bakhuizen van den Brink, "Traditio im theolo-
gischen Sinn," *Vigiliae Christianae* 13 (1959): 65–86.

5. In addition to the texts of Varro already cited in the previous note,
see also *The City of God* IV, 31: "Those who first set up images of the gods
for the people both reduced reverence and increased error in their
cities" (Babcock, *Augustine* I, 140); and likewise ibid., IV, 9. On Scaevo-

la, see ibid., IV, 27: "It is recorded that the pontiff Scaevola, whose literary knowledge was immense, argued that three views of the gods are passed down to us: one by the poets, another by the philosophers, and a third by political leaders. The first, he says, is mere nonsense, because many disgraceful tales have been made up about the gods, and the second is not suitable for civic society, because some things it contains are superfluous and some are even harmful for the people to know. The superfluous matters are no great issue, for, as the common-place among jurists goes, 'Superfluous things do no harm.' But what are the points that actually do harm when they are made known to the multitude? They are, he says, such statements as these: 'That Hercules, Aesculapius, Castor, and Pollux are not gods, for the learned claim that these were men who passed beyond our human condition.' What else? 'That cities do not have true images of the gods, for the true god has neither sex nor age nor defined body parts.' The pontiff does not want the people to know these things because, in fact, he does not consider them to be false. Clearly, then, his view is that it is expedient for cities to be deceived in matters of religion" (Babcock, *Augustine* I, 134–35). Augustine cites Seneca's position vis-à-vis the cult of the state, ibid. VI, 10: "The wise man will observe all these rites not because they are pleasing to the gods but because they are enjoined by law"; and a few lines later: "As for all that ignoble throng of gods assembled through the ages by ancient superstition, we will adore them, but only with the reminder that their worship has far more to do with custom than with truth" (Babcock, *Augustine* I, 204). The citations from Seneca are taken from a lost work entitled *On Superstition*. On Augustine's relationship to Seneca, see *Bibliothèque Augustinienne* 34, 571–72. On the official cult and interior religion, see ibid., 572–74, with numerous references to Cicero.

the sake of tradition. Concern for the *polis* and its
well-being justified the violation of truth. In other
words, the well-being of the state, which was believed to be dependent on the continuance of its ancient forms, was more highly valued than the truth.

It was here that Augustine saw one of the great
distinctions between Rome and Christianity in
all its acuity: In the Roman understanding, religion was an institution of the state and hence a
function of the state; as such it was subordinate
to the state. It was not an absolute that was independent of the interests of the various groups that
professed it; rather, its value was dependent on
its serviceability vis-à-vis the state, which was the
absolute. In the Christian understanding, on the
other hand, religion had to do not with custom but
with truth, which was absolute. It was, therefore,
not instituted by the state but rather had itself instituted a new community that embraced everyone
who lived in God's truth.[6] From that perspective

6. See *The City of God* VI, 4: "Varro himself states that he wrote first

Augustine understood the Christian faith as a freeing—namely, a freeing from the tyranny of custom
for the sake of the truth.[7]

The Power of the Demons

The political religion of the Romans, to
be sure, did not possess any truth, but there
was a truth that hovered over it, and this truth was
that the enslavement of man to untruthful cus-

---

about human matters and only then about divine matters, because
cities came into existence first, and then these rites were instituted
by them. The true religion, however, was not instituted by any earthly
city; instead, clearly, the true religion itself instituted the heavenly
city" (Babcock, *Augustine* I, 190).

7. See ibid., IV, 30: "Let us Christians, therefore, give thanks to the
Lord our God . . . who, through the supreme humility of Christ . . . and
through the faith of the martyrs who died for the truth and now live
with the truth, has overthrown these superstitions by the free service
of his people . . . not only in the hearts of the religious but also in the
very temples of the superstitious" (Babcock, *Augustine* I, 139). Ibid., VI,
2: "What should we make of this, except that a man of the greatest acu-
men and learning [i.e., Varro] (although not set free by the Holy Spirit)
was obliged to submit to the laws and customs of his city?" (Babcock,
Augustine I, 188, alt.)

toms had delivered him over to the ungodly powers that the Christian faith called demons; to that degree the worship of idols was not merely a foolish and baseless affectation but, in its delivering over of man to the renunciation of truth, had become the worship of demons. This was Augustine's second fundamental assertion.

Behind the ineffectual gods stood the highly effectual power of the demons,[8] and behind the enslavement to custom stood enslavement to evil spirits. Herein lay the true depth of Christian freeing and the freedom that had been gained in it. Inasmuch as this freedom set a person free from custom, it freed him from a power that man had in fact himself created, but which long before had outgrown him and now lorded it over him, which had turned into an objective power that was independent of him, into an opening for the power

8. This affirmation can be found throughout the first part of *The City of God*. What follows is a nonexhaustive selection of texts: IV, 1, 27, 29, 31; V, 12, 18, 24; VI, 4; VIII, 14 (fundamental), 18; IX, 3, 8–9.

of evil as such that was overwhelming him, which was called "demons." Being freed from custom for the sake of the truth meant being freed from the power of the demons that hid behind custom.[9] At this point the sacrifice of Christ and of Christians now became truly understandable as redemption—in other words, as a setting free. It overthrew the political cult that was opposed to truth and replaced the political cult, which was a cult

9. See ibid., IV, 31: "How vast and how malign the power of the demons is—the power from which we are set free by the unique sacrifice of the holy blood shed for us and the gift of the Spirit bestowed on us" (Babcock, *Augustine* I, 140). Ibid., V, 18: "If a father [i.e., the Roman Junius Brutus, who opposed King Tarquin] could kill his sons for the sake of liberty for men who were going to die in any case, and for the sake of desire for the praises that we gain from mortal men, is it any great thing if, for the sake of the true liberty which sets us free from the dominion of iniquity and death and the devil, we do not kill our sons but simply count Christ's poor among our sons? It is not from desire for human praise that we do this but from love of setting people free—free not from a King Tarquin but from the demons and from the prince of demons" (Babcock, *Augustine* I, 167–68). Ibid., IX, 15: "on those whose hearts he purifies by faith and has delivered from their foul dominion" (Babcock, *Augustine* I, 293).

of demons, with the one universal service of the truth, which was freedom.[10]

Here Augustine's thinking coincides with that of Origen. Just as Origen had understood the religious absolutizing of national identity as the work of the demonic angels of the peoples, and the supranational unity of Christians as the being set free from the prison of "the people," so Augustine viewed the political from the perspective of Antiquity—namely, as the divinization of the *polis*, albeit in the sense of its demonization—and saw in Christianity the overcoming of the demonic power of the political, which had suppressed the truth. For him, likewise, the pagan gods were not mere illusions but the fantastic masks behind which real powers and forces were hidden, which denied man access to absolute values by enclosing him in relativity, and the domain of the political was the actual domain of these powers. Augustine certain-

10. See Ratzinger, *Volk und Haus Gottes in Augustins Lehre von der Kirche*, 188–234.

ly allowed for the truth of Euhemerus's idea—that all the gods were originally once human beings and that hence the whole of pagan religion was founded on an exaggeration of human worth— while at the same time seeing that this idea by no means solved the riddle of the pagan religions. The powers that people apparently thought came from within themselves soon showed themselves to be objective forces, or demons, that exercised a very real domination over them.[11] Only God himself, the power over all powers, could free human beings from them.[12]

11. Augustine touches briefly on the problem of euhemerism in connection with the theses of Scaevola in *The City of God* IV, 27. There is a more extended treatment (with a reference to Euhemerus), ibid., VI, 7; and an especially detailed one in connection with Hermes Trismegistos, ibid., VIII, 26. In all these instances his explanations fall back on the idea of the demonic. See also *Bibliothèque Augustinienne* 33, 785; 34, 585–86.
12. On the concept of freedom, or liberation, see notes 7 and 9 in this chapter. See further the debate with Porphyry on the concept of purification in *The City of God* X, 24–32, well summarized at 32: "This is the religion that contains the universal way of the soul's liberation, for no soul can be liberated by any other way" (Babcock, *Augustine* I, 344).

The Starting Point for the Augustinian Theology of the Political

A question remains as to what positive theology of the political Augustine can offer after so many negative statements. Here as well his reflections were developed over against the two most important political philosophies of his time, Stoicism and Platonism.

The Antithesis of the Stoa

Stoic monism had allowed for the whole world to be viewed as saturated with divinity and, correspondingly, for the places where its power was especially concentrated to be given the qualifier "divine." Understandably the political theology of the Romans seized hold of this particular concept (from which it very quickly derived the right of the state), in order to identify itself as the norm and source of religion.[13] Augustine set

13. Consequently it is understandable that Varro, in his search for a phil-

his Christian faith in creation over against the monism of the Stoa: "In the true theology, the earth is the work of God, not his mother."[14] The world contained in itself nothing absolute. It was entirely God's creation and his work; the absolute was beyond it, not in it.

The Antithesis of Platonism

If Stoicism meant the mingling of God and the world and thus the abolition of transcendence, Platonism, on the contrary, was marked by a radical exaggeration of transcendence: God had nothing to do with the world.[15] For Augus-

---

osophical basis, found it in Stoicism. Augustine features his definition of the concept of God, ibid., IV, 31. On the origins and effect of his threefold concept of theology, which was analyzed in depth by Augustine, see J. Pépin, "La 'théologie tripartite' de Varron: Essai de reconstitution et recherche de sources," *Revue des Etudes Augustiniennes* 2 (1956): 265–94. See also *Bibliothèque Augustinienne* 33, 813; 34, 565. Pépin, "La 'théologie tripartite,'" 269–78, offers a fine analysis of the extant writings of Scaevola.

14. *The City of God* VI, 8 (Babcock, *Augustine* I, 197, alt.).

15. See note 2 in this chapter. For an extensive discussion see *Bibliothèque Augustinienne* 34, 612–14.

tine, who believed in the incarnation of God, this dogma was untenable. God made the world, and it only existed by reason of the fact that he attended to it. No worldly material was contaminated, and no creature was unworthy of God or able to reach him only through intermediaries. The only contaminated thing was a mind turned against God, and alienation from God came from a spiritual rejection of him.[16] The foundational Platonic dogma, "Between God and man there is no contact,"[17] was for Augustine replaced by the objective fact, wit-

16. See *The City of God* IX, 17, where Augustine conflates and slightly alters Plotinus, *Enneads* I, 6, 8; II, 3: "We must flee, therefore, to our beloved homeland. Our Father is there; all is there. What ship are we to use, then, what means of flight? We must become like God." To this Augustine adds: "If it is true that the more a person is like God, the closer he is to God, then the only way to be distant from God is to be unlike him." Particularly noteworthy is the statement at the end of the same chapter: "And meanwhile there are two matters of no small importance that he showed us, for our salvation, by his incarnation—that true divinity cannot be contaminated by the flesh, and that we should not think that the demons are superior to us just because they do not have flesh" (Babcock, *Augustine* I, 297).

17. Ibid., IX, 16, cited above on page 72.

nessed to by Christian faith, that God had become man.[18] God, who had created the world, also remained its Lord; the Creator God was also the God of history. From this realization sprang the leitmotiv of Augustine's political theology: *Ipse dat regna terrena*.[19] It is God himself who distributes earthly kingdoms. The political world, with its manifold and opposing states, had no special divinities but rather was subordinate to the one God, whose works were creation and history.

18. In *Confessions* VIII, Augustine describes how an acknowledgement of the *descensus Dei*, the descent of God into our human condition, contributed to his going beyond Platonism. Over the course of his life he saw there the real difference between Christianity and mere philosophizing. See Ratzinger, *Volk und Haus Gottes in Augustins Lehre von der Kirche*, 2–12.

19. *The City of God* IV, 33. See also ibid., V, 1: "It is beyond doubt . . . that human kingdoms are established by divine providence" (Babcock, *Augustine* I, 144). See *Bibliothèque Augustinienne* 33, 767–69.

The Theological Use of the Old Testament and of Roman History

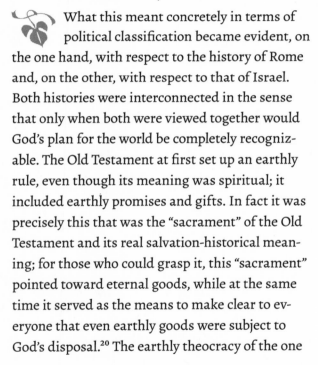 What this meant concretely in terms of political classification became evident, on the one hand, with respect to the history of Rome and, on the other, with respect to that of Israel. Both histories were interconnected in the sense that only when both were viewed together would God's plan for the world be completely recognizable. The Old Testament at first set up an earthly rule, even though its meaning was spiritual; it included earthly promises and gifts. In fact it was precisely this that was the "sacrament" of the Old Testament and its real salvation-historical meaning; for those who could grasp it, this "sacrament" pointed toward eternal goods, while at the same time it served as the means to make clear to everyone that even earthly goods were subject to God's disposal.[20] The earthly theocracy of the one

20. See *The City of God* IV, 33: "And this is the sacrament of the Old

God was established in Israel as a sign in world history, which indicated that there was no division between so-called high religion and political religion but rather that God's rule was one and that it encompassed all human beings and all areas of human existence.

This Old Testament message, however, was enlarged and expanded by the knowledge that was gained from the history of Rome. Here, of course, idolaters possessed a vast measure of earthly goods and earthly success. But it had to be that way. On the one hand, God had given his own people in Israel earthly rule in order to show that this too came from him. On the other, he had given demon-worshipers—first in the great Eastern kingdoms

Testament, where the New Testament was hidden—that, in the Old Testament, the promises and gifts are of earthly things, although even then spiritual men understood (but did not yet openly proclaim) both the eternity signified by those temporal things and which of God's gifts are the ones that bring true happiness" (Babcock, *Augustine* I,141, alt.). The theme is continued, ibid., IV, 34. See also *Bibliothèque Augustinienne* 33, 814–17.

and then in Rome—earthly power in order to show
that none of this possessed any ultimate value
but rather was something entirely penultimate,
which man had to outgrow so as to arrive at his
true goal. "The one true God himself gives earthly
kingdoms to the good and to the evil alike. . . . As
for [true] happiness, he gives this only to the good.
Slaves can have or not have happiness, and rulers can have or not have happiness, although full
happiness will come only in the life where no one
will be a slave any longer. And the reason why God
gives earthly kingdoms to the good and the evil
alike is this: to keep his worshipers, who are still no
more advanced in mind than little children, from
yearning for this gift from him as if it were some
great thing."[21] Hence, earthly rule in the hands of
the good and the bad was the divine sign in history
with a double meaning that pointed both to God's

---

21. *The City of God* IV, 33 (Babcock, *Augustine* I, 141). On the succession of
kingdoms from East to West, see ibid., V, 13.

absolute power and to the relativity of this-worldly values, and especially of political entities.

The history of Rome as an earthly state in which the history of the world was ultimately gathered up permitted a deeper understanding of these facts. First there was the history of the Roman republic, which was able to push its frontiers to the ends of the earth. Rome's good fortune in this respect gave greater exposure to the same dialectic that lay behind every earthly institution. The basis for Rome's success, in Augustine's eyes, was the *prisca virtus Romana*, ancient Roman virtue. But what really was this Roman virtue? To use Virgil's definition, it consisted in *amor patriae laudumque immensa cupido*, "love of country and immense desire for praise."[22] It was a renunciation of other burdens for the sake of the one burden of boundless patriotic ambition and the will to power. Thus, the Romans were good "within the context of the

22. *Aeneid* VI, 823, cited in *The City of God* V, 18.

earthly city"—good, in other words, if a nation's earthly greatness were taken to be the highest value.[23] Their virtue represented a renunciation of many vices for the sake of a single vice, namely, the absolutization of the nation.[24] So it was only

23. *The City of God* V, 19 (Babcock, *Augustine* I, 172). See also ibid., V, 12: "We can see what they wanted virtue to culminate in, and what the good among them correlated virtue with, namely, honor. . . . Therefore virtue should not follow on the glory, honor and power which the Romans desired for themselves and which the good among them strove to attain by 'good arts.' . . . For there is no true virtue except the virtue that is directed toward the end where man's good is actually found, the good than which there is no better" (Babcock, *Augustine* I, 161–62). Ibid., V, 13: "Nevertheless, it is for the better that people who do not restrain their baser lusts by the pious faith and the love of intelligible beauty that are given by the Holy Spirit at least do so by their desire for human praise and glory. They certainly are not saints, but at least they are less vile" (Babcock, *Augustine* I, 163).

24. See ibid., V, 13: "Who, for the sake of honor, praise and glory, served the good of the country in which they sought their own glory and did not hesitate to put its well-being above their own. For the sake of this one vice—that is, the love of praise—these men suppressed the love of riches and many other vices" (Babcock, *Augustine* I, 163). Ibid., V, 14: "But since these Romans belonged to an earthly city, and since the goal set before them in all their services on its behalf was to secure its safety

right that what they so ardently strove for and
were prepared to sacrifice everything for was actually granted them: national greatness. But what
was bestowed on them by a just God was at the
same time their punishment. They had made the
nation's earthly greatness their highest value and
had thereby cut themselves off from something
greater, the values of eternity. They belonged to
those persons of whom the Lord said: "Truly, I say
to you, they have received their reward" (Mt 6:2).[25]
They had sought and obtained an earthly kingdom
in place of an eternal kingdom, and earthly promi-
nence in place of eternal glory. The Roman Empire,
the sign of its greatness, was simultaneously the
sign of their eternal rejection. That was the sober

and to gain a kingdom not in heaven but on earth, not in eternal life
but in a life where the dying pass away and are succeeded by those who
are going to die in turn, what else was there for them to love but glory?
And what glory but the glory by which they yearned to find a life after
death, as it were, on the lips of those who praised them?" (Babcock,
Augustine I, 165).

25. See ibid., V, 15.

judgment of the bishop of Hippo regarding the splendor that had blinded others' eyes. Rome ultimately became a moral example for Augustine: the immense effort that people had committed to the transitory goal of an earthly state and earthly greatness should provide a powerful impetus for the believer to spend all his energies on the eternal goal that had become visible and accessible for him in the person of Christ Jesus.[26]

The republic was followed by the imperial age in Rome, and that too had double significance, inasmuch as it produced both a Nero and a Constantine. Nero himself, the epitome of everything horrible, had possessed power over a world empire. "But even in the case of men such as these, the power to dominate is given only by the providence of the supreme God, when he judges that the state

---

26. There are wonderful applications of Roman virtue to Christian life, ibid., V, 18. See E. von Ivanka, "Römische Ideologie in der 'Civitas Dei,'" in Congrès International Augustinien, *Augustinus Magister* III (Paris, 1955), 411–17; *Bibliothèque Augustinienne* 33, 830–31.

of human affairs deserves such overlords."[27] This was a powerful statement made by a man who had an unvarnished understanding of human wickedness and who spoke about it in an unvarnished way. And he who had previously always offered the *prisca virtus Romana* as the reason for Roman greatness added reflectively: "As best I could, then, I have explained why the one true and just God aided the Romans in obtaining the glory of such a great empire, for they were good men within the context of the earthly city. It is possible, of course, that there is another more hidden reason, better known to God than to us, which has to do with the diverse merits of humankind."[28] Who knows, Augustine seems to want to say, whether the Roman

27. *The City of God* V, 19 (Babcock, *Augustine* I, 172). Augustine adds to this two scriptural proofs: "By me kings reign, and by me tyrants hold the earth" (Prv 8:15), which he admits could be translated differently than in the Latin version that he had before him, and so he cites a further text: "He causes the hypocrite to reign on account of the perversity of the people" (Jb 34:30).

28. Ibid. (Babcock, *Augustine* I, 172).

Empire throughout its history, and not merely
the relatively brief moment when Nero ruled it,
was perhaps God's scourge, which we should turn
away from with a shudder instead of foolishly
admiring?

Yet along with Nero there was also Constantine,
and this fact as well excluded any one-sided insis-
tence on viewing the political in demonic terms.
It was certainly true that political power had been
given over to the minions of the demons in order
to demonstrate its low value, but it was God who
had given it over, and he had from time to time
also given it to those who belonged to him in order
to show that he was Lord and that he did as he
wished. The political and military good fortune of
a Constantine and of a Theodosius indicated that
one did not have to flee to the demons in order to
acquire such gifts. The political was not necessarily
demonic, and it did not necessarily draw its life
from lying and from a disdain for justice; it could
also flourish in the soil of truth and righteous-

ness.[29] But a Christian would not call the Christian
emperors happy because of their political success.
"Rather, we call them happy if they rule justly; if
they do not swell with pride among the voices of
those who honor them too highly and the obsequi-
ousness of those who acclaim them too humbly,
but remember that they are only human beings; if
they make their power the servant of God's majes-
ty, using it to spread the worship of God as much
as possible; if they fear, love, and worship God; if,
more than their own kingdom, they love the one
where they do not fear to have co-rulers; if they are
slow to punish and quick to pardon; if they enforce
punishment only as necessary for governing and
defending the republic, not to satisfy their per-
sonal animosities; if they grant pardon not to let
wrongdoing go unpunished but in the hope of its
being corrected; if they compensate for the harsh
decisions that they are often compelled to make

29. See ibid., V, 24–26.

with the leniency of mercy and the generosity of beneficence; if the more they are in a position to give free rein to self-indulgence the more they hold it in check; if they prefer to govern their own base desires more than to govern any peoples; if they do all this not out of a craving for empty glory but rather out of love for eternal happiness; and if, for their sins, they do not neglect to offer their true God the sacrifice of humility and compassion and prayer."[30]

In this Christian "mirror of princes" there appears—for us in a way that is particularly moving—the admonition that the emperor, even as emperor, is supposed to remain a human being. Political or national greatness and power became in Augustine's portrayal a kind of mask, behind which

---

30. Ibid., V, 24 (Babcock, *Augustine* I, 178, alt.). On Augustine's notion of sacrifice, as it appears at the end of this passage, see J. Lécuyer, "Le sacrifice selon saint Augustin," in *Augustinus Magister* II (Paris, 1954), 905–14; J. Ratzinger, "Originalität und Überlieferung in Augustins Begriff der confessio," *Revue des Etudes Augustiniennes* 3 (1957): 375–92, esp. 389–92.

in the end there stood only a human being. That
was especially clear when he cried out to Rome,
the world's proud mistress, "Cease your boasting!
What are all men, after all, but men?"[31] The devaluation of national greatness opened the way to see
what was common to humanity. Human-beingness
was not, as it could appear at first, merely the shab-
by residue that was concealed behind the glittering
facades of earthly power; it was in fact a positive
reality that deserved to be brought forth from
behind these facades. That could be seen when
humanitas and *gratia*, humanity and grace, were
mentioned in the same breath, and the person who
acted in a human way appeared as someone who
acted with simple and indubitable greatness.[32] It
was *gratissime et humanissime*, "most graciously and
humanely," that one day—much too late!—

31. *The City of God* V, 17.
32. See ibid., V, 26: "He took Valentinian under his wing, preserved his
imperial dignity, and consoled him with *humanity and grace*" (Babcock,
Augustine I, 179, alt.). Ibid., V, 17: "And this would have been especially

the Roman Empire made all its inhabitants citizens of Rome and thus recognized that common human identity far outweighed a previous concern with boundaries established by force of arms.[33]

The Place of the Church in History

The actual driving force for the devaluation of the political, however, lay (in contrast to Stoic cosmopolitanism) not in this emphasis on the unity of human beings; that was, rather, merely the consequence of the spiritual and intellectual movement which shaped the whole of Augustine's thought—namely, the discovery of "the fatherland on high."[34] For Augustine earthly states

true if the Romans had immediately taken the *most gracious and humane* action that they took later on, when they granted civic standing to all who belonged to the Roman Empire so that they would be Roman citizens" (Babcock, *Augustine* I, 166).

33. See ibid., V, 17.

34. See ibid., V, 16: The expansion of the Roman Empire "also happened for the citizens of that eternal city while they are on pilgrimage here

and earthly fatherlands held second place, since
he had found God's state, and in it was the one fa-

---

below. It happened so that they might carefully and soberly contemplate the Roman examples, and might see how great a love they owe to their supernal *fatherland* for the sake of eternal life, if the earthly city was so greatly loved by its citizens for the sake of mere human glory." (Babcock, *Augustine* I, 166, alt.) Ibid., V, 17: "The city in which it is promised that we shall reign is as far removed from this one as heaven is from earth. . . . The citizens of such a marvelous *fatherland* should not think that they have done anything remarkable if, for the sake of attaining it, they performed some good work. . . . And this point is especially noteworthy because the remission of sins, which gathers citizens for the eternal *fatherland*, has a kind of likeness, a sort of shadow, in the asylum established by Romulus, where impunity for every sort of crime brought together the multitude that was to found the city of Rome." (Babcock, *Augustine* I, 167, alt.) Ibid., V, 18: "Is it any great thing, then, to despise all the enticements of this world, no matter how alluring they may be, for the sake of the eternal and heavenly *fatherland*, when, for the sake of his temporal and earthly country, Brutus was even able to kill his own sons?" (Babcock, *Augustine* I, 167, alt.) Ibid.: "If Regulus could do this [i.e., allow himself to be tortured for the sake of Rome], are there any tortures that should not be despised for the sake of keeping faith with the *fatherland* to whose blessedness faith itself leads?" (Babcock, *Augustine* I, 169, alt.) Examples of the Christian appropriation of the pagan concept of *patria*, "fatherland" or "homeland," would be easy to multiply.

therland of all men. No one should succumb to any illusion here: all the states on earth were "earthly states," even when they were ruled by Christian emperors and inhabited more or less only by Christian citizens. Since they were states on this earth they were "earthly states," and they could not be anything else.[35] As such they were the inevitable

35. That the *civitas terrena* or *regnum terrenum*, the "earthly city/state" or the "earthly kingdom," refers simply to the states of this earth and to their history, including those inhabited and ruled by Christians, can be shown from numerous texts. One need only mention ibid., V, 19 (Augustine had previously mentioned that true virtue could only exist in tandem with the true worship of God, and he now wanted to say that persons who, like the ancient Romans, possessed a merely political and hence relative virtue were more useful to the state than those who did not possess even as much as that): "Those who are not citizens of the eternal city (which is called the city of God in our Sacred Scriptures) are more useful to the earthly city when they at least have the kind of virtue that serves human glory than when they do not" (Babcock, *Augustine* I, 172–73). See also, *inter alia*, ibid., V, 1; V, 12; V, 14; V, 19; V, 25; VI, 1. There are extensive citations in F. E. Cranz, "'De civitate Dei' XV, 2 et l'idée augustinienne de la société chrétienne," *Revue des Etudes Augustiniennes* 3 (1957): 15–27; Ratzinger, *Volk und Haus Gottes in Augustins Lehre von der Kirche*, 281–95, esp. note 82.

products of this world-age, and it was right to care for their well-being. Augustine himself loved the Roman state as his fatherland, and he was lovingly concerned with its existence.[36] But, inasmuch as all such structures once were and still continued to be earthly states, they had only a relative value and were not worthy of ultimate concern. Ultimate concern had to do only with the eternal homeland of all human beings, the *civitas caelestis*, the "heavenly city."

Here too we find Augustine in agreement with

---

36. Particularly indicative in this regard is the kind of spontaneous remark, for example, that one can find in *The City of God* IV, 7, in this case with respect to the recent sack of Rome: "The Roman Empire . . . is simply afflicted, not changed into something else. The same thing has happened to it in other eras, before Christ's name was proclaimed, and it has recovered from such affliction. There is no need, then, to despair of recovery now" (Babcock, *Augustine* I, 115). For an extensive treatment of this issue, see J. Straub, "Augustinus Sorge um die Regeneratio Imperii. Das Imperium Romanum als Civitas terrena," *Historisches Jahrbuch* 73 (1954): 34–60; and also *Bibliothèque Augustinienne* 33,791–92. F. G. Maier, *Augustin und das antike Rom* (Stuttgart, 1955), is insistent on the anti-Roman thrust of Augustine's writings.

Origen and with the entire Christian tradition, when he is convinced that *civitas caelestis* is an apt name not only for the coming heavenly Jerusalem but also and even now for the people of God on their pilgrimage through the desert of the earthly age—in other words, for the Church.[37] In it is assembled from all times and peoples, from beyond the borders of the Roman Empire, the community of those who, together with God's holy angels, will form a single eternal *polis*.[38] On this earth, of

37. On this much-discussed question, see the comprehensive and very clear proofs indicated in Cranz 22ff. From the numerous texts a few examples can be cited: *The City of God* XIII, 16: "But the philosophers against whose slanders we are defending the city of God—that is, his Church" (Babcock, *Augustine* II, 80). Ibid., XVI, 2: "Christ and his Church, which is the city of God" (Babcock, *Augustine* II, 187). Ibid., VIII, 24: "A house is now being built for the Lord in all the earth— namely, the city of God, which is the holy Church" (Babcock, *Augustine* I, 272). From the perspective of what these texts demonstrate, there is nothing more amazing than the ongoing denial of the equivalence of the Church and the city of God in the literature that has been influenced by idealistic thought.

38. On Augustine's universalism, which ignores the boundaries

course, it lives as an alien, and it can never live in
any other way, because its true place is elsewhere.

So it was that the states of the world would remain earthly states until the end of the ages, and
that the Church would remain an alien community—likewise until the end of the ages. This was
evident in the fact that the Church, in keeping with
its essence, was a Church of martyrs. Augustine's
theology of martyrdom was an essential part of
his theology of the Church, the entity that stood
over against the state, which took its life from demons. This becomes clear when he explains that
the martyr is the Christian opposite of the pagan
Heros. According to mythology, Heros was the son
of Hera, the Greek goddess whose Roman equiva-
lent was Juno. She was the mythological personi-
fication of what we would now call inner space (in

---

imposed by the Roman empire, see Peterson, "Der Monotheismus als
politisches Problem," 146–47, note 5. On his temporal universalism, see
Y. Congar, "Ecclesia ab Abel," in M. Reding, ed., *Abhandlungen über Theologie und Kirche: Festschrift Karl Adam* (Düsseldorf, 1952), 79–108.

contrast to outer space), which was viewed as the abode of the demons. Demons, then, were beings that dwelled in the air; they constituted an anonymous power associated with a particular spiritual climate in accordance with which a person would direct his life and by which he would let himself be ruled.[39] Heros, who belonged to Hera and who was raised into the air, was a human being who was no longer merely a human being. It was he who determined the spiritual climate, the "air," in which one breathed and lived. He was no longer merely a human being but had obtained power, was raised up to the "principalities and powers" (Col 2:15) by which human beings have allowed themselves to

39. See *The City of God* X, 21. I have attempted to reproduce the sense of the Augustinian (and generally patristic) assertion that the air was the abode of the demons in such a way as to be comprehensible to modern thinking. On this see Schlier, *Mächte und Gewalten im Neuen Testament*, 28ff. Of course this existential sense was not always understood primarily in a cosmological way. But Schlier has shown that the New Testament knew it, and that Augustine recognized it is evident throughout his discussion of the problem of the demonic in *The City of God* I–X.

be led, and became a demon.[40] The Christian martyr, on the other hand, was one who did not act in
accordance with these powers, as was customary,
but who, rather, defeated them thanks to his faith
in God's greater power. His victory consisted in
suffering and in saying "no" to the powers that
governed the majority of people.[41] Augustine saw

40. See *The City of God* X, 21: "This term is said to be derived from Juno,
since Juno is called Hera in Greek; and therefore, according to Greek
myth, one of her sons was named Heros. In some mystic fashion, this
myth supposedly signifies that the air is reckoned as Juno's province,
and that is where people say heroes dwell, along with the demons. By
'heroes' they mean the souls of the dead marked by some special merit"
(Babcock, *Augustine* I, 328–29).

41. See ibid. for the continuation of the text from the previous note: "In
contrast, our martyrs would be called heroes (if, as I said, ecclesiastical usage allowed) not because they are joined in community with the
demons in the air but because they defeated those very same demons—
that is, those powers of the air—including Juno herself, no matter what
she is supposed to signify" (Babcock, *Augustine* I, 329). Augustine then
points to the fact that the pagans try to pacify bad demons through gifts,
and he continues, ibid.: "This is not the way of true and holy religion.
This is not how our martyrs defeat Juno, that is, the powers of the air. . . .
Our heroes (if usage allowed us to call them that) do not overcome Hera
with suppliant gifts but with divine virtues" (Babcock, *Augustine* I, 329).

in martyrdom the particular aspect of Christian victory in this world-age, and in the martyr he saw the sign of the Church, which lived and conquered in this world under the form of suffering.

The bishop of Hippo thus came to terms not only with the reality of and even the necessity for the state but also with its imperfection—or, more correctly, with the imperfection of all the states— in this world. To that extent the eschatological radicalness of the Christian revolution is considerably more measured in him than it is in Origen. The difference in their positions is also evident in their conception of the unification of humanity. Both Origen and Augustine followed the Late Jewish and early Christian tradition of seeing the division of humanity into nations primarily from the perspective of the problem of language: human beings were unavoidably cut off from one another by the vast number of different languages.[42] Both Origen

42. For proofs of this, see Peterson, "Das Problem des Nationalismus im alten Christentum," 61–62, and note 35.

and Augustine saw in this confusion of languages the sign of the sinfulness that was to be conquered in Christ Jesus. For his part, Origen's gaze went immediately to the *eschaton*, when everyone would speak a single language; at that point the unity of humanity would be reestablished. The unity of language was an exclusively eschatological gift; only at the *eschaton* would the hope for it be fulfilled.[43]

Augustine viewed the issue differently. He very emphatically set the miracle of the tongues at Pentecost (Acts 2:1–13) over against the Babylonian confusion of languages. But, while for Origen the miracle of Pentecost remained a onetime eschatological sign, Augustine saw in it a kind of symbol of what was happening in the Church on an ongoing basis—namely, that the one Church encompassed all lands and languages and that the community of love for the Lord embraced those who were linguistically separated from one another. In the body of

43. See ibid., 62, note 35. On the mystical-spiritualizing interpretation that Origen gives along with the eschatological, see note 47.

Christ, where all languages were spoken, the miracle of Pentecost was an enduring phenomenon. In Augustine's words:

> Why are you unwilling to speak in the languages of all? Every tongue resounded there. How is it that today a person to whom the Holy Spirit has been given does not speak in the tongues of all? At that date it was a sign that the Holy Spirit had come upon people when they spoke in all languages. What are you going to say now, you heretic? That the Holy Spirit is not given? ... But if he is given, why do those to whom he is given not speak in the tongues of all peoples? ... Why then does the Holy Spirit not manifest himself today in the multiplicity of languages? But he does; he is manifest today in all tongues. At the beginning the Church was not spread throughout the entire world, making it possible for Christ's members to speak among all nations, and therefore the miracle happened in each person as a presage of what would later

be true of all. Today the whole body of Christ does speak in the languages of all peoples, or, rather, if there are any tongues in which it does not yet speak, it will. The Church will grow until it claims all languages as its own. . . . I dare to say to you, "I speak in the tongues of all. I am in Christ's body, I am in Christ's Church. If Christ's body today speaks in the languages of all, I too speak in all languages. Greek is mine, Syriac is mine, Hebrew is mine. Mine is the tongue of every nation, because I am within the unity that embraces all nations."[44]

What that tower [of Babel] had disunited the Church is bringing together. Many tongues were made out of one; do not be surprised, pride did this. One tongue is being made out of many; do not be surprised, charity did this.[45]

---

44. *Exposition of Psalm* 147, 19, translated by M. Boulding, *The Works of Saint Augustine* III, 20 (Hyde Park, N.Y., 2004), 464, alt.
45. *Homily on the Gospel of John* 6, 10, translated by E. Hill, *The Works of Saint Augustine* III, 12 (Hyde Park, N.Y. 2009), 130.

For Augustine, becoming a Christian essentially meant going from a scattered existence to unity, from the Tower of Babel to the upper room of Pentecost, from the many peoples of the human race to one new people.[46]

It would be an attractive project, but one too ambitious for the present essay, to compare these two theologies of language—Origen's eschatological theology (which is joined in his writings to a time-transcending mystical, spiritualizing theology)[47]

46. See Ratzinger, *Volk und Haus Gottes in Augustins Lehre von der Kirche*, 127–58, esp. note 82, which indicates with numerous references how, in his debate with the Donatists, Augustine was increasingly drawn to see the core of Christian existence in that concrete *caritas* by way of which *omnes gentes* would be brought together into *una gens*. One text may suffice for the many that could be adduced. See *Answer to the Letters of Petilian* III, 3, 4: "And when they [i.e., the Donatists] flee from communion with those men [i.e., immoral Catholics], as persons whom they know, they are abandoning unity with it [i.e., the Church], when, if the charity that endures all things were in them (1 Cor 13:7), they would instead put up with what they know in one nation (*una gente*), lest they cut themselves off from the good to whom, among all the nations (*omnibus gentibus*), they were unable to teach alien and bad things."
47. See *Against Celsus* VIII, 22: The Christian "is always living in the

and Augustine's ecclesiastical-sacramental theolo-gy[48]—with the third one that was developed along the political-theocratic lines set down by Eusebius of Caesarea, according to which the eschatological uni-fication of languages was accomplished in the unity of the imperial language of New Rome.[49] Eusebius's theology is significant in that it equated Christian

---

days of Pentecost, and particularly when, like the apostles of Jesus, he goes up to the upper room and gives time to supplication and prayer, so that he becomes worthy of the mighty rushing wind from heaven which compels the evil in men and its consequences to disappear, and so that he becomes worthy also of some share in the fiery tongue given by God" (Chadwick, *Origen*, 468). See also idem, *Homily on Jeremiah* 20, 1–7. This style of interpretation lies on a purely individual and interior level, whereas, in *Against Celsus* V, 29–31, the visibly developing hope in a unified language is purely eschatological. The eschatological concept of a unification of language is clearer in Filastrius of Brescia, *A Book of the Various Heresies*, 76–77. Augustine's ecclesiastical interpretation thus stands in the middle between a purely mystical and spiritualizing approach on the one hand, and a purely eschatological approach on the other.

48. One may speak of a sacramental understanding inasmuch as, for Augustine, *caritas* is closely connected to *communio*. See Ratzinger, *Volk und Haus Gottes in Augustins Lehre von der Kirche*, 136–58, esp. note 82.

49. See the texts cited in Peterson, "Das Problem des Nationalismus

universalism with Rome's universal empire; in so
doing it dragged down that universalism to a political level and thus robbed it of its breadth and depth.
The door had now been opened to nationalism,
which was once again able to fix itself on an actual political entity.[50] In Augustine, in contrast, the
newness that Christianity introduced was evident.
His doctrine of two states, or cities, aimed neither
at a state dominated by the Church nor at a Church
dominated by the state. Its goal, rather, was—in
the midst of the structures of this world, which
remained and indeed had to remain what they

---

im alten Christentum," 62, note 35. Peterson refers to O. Treitinger, *Die
oströmische Kaiser- und Reichsidee* (Jena, 1938), 165.

50. On the imperial theology of Eusebius, see Peterson, "Der Monotheismus als politisches Problem," 86–93, note 5; Cranz, "'De civitate Dei'
XV, 2 et l'idée augustinienne de la société chrétienne," 24–27, note 107,
which lists further literature. A well thought-out and more positive
view of the theology that originated with Eusebius is offered in E. von
Ivanka, *Rhomäerreich und Gottesvolk* (Freiburg, 1968). Ivanka empha-
sizes the Old Testament components of the Byzantine idea of empire,
which in no way can be understood simply as a Christian development
of the pagan concept of the empire ruled by a divine emperor.

were—to offer the new power of faith in the unity of men within the body of Christ as an element of a transformation whose ultimate form would be shaped by God himself, when history had finally completed its course.

Conclusion

In conclusion it is important to note that Augustine himself did not attempt to work out what a world that had embraced Christianity would look like. His city of God, to be sure, is not a purely ideal community composed entirely of all the people who believe in God, but neither does it have anything to do with an earthly theocracy, with a world that is established along Christian lines; it is, rather, a sacramental-eschatological entity, which lives in this world as a sign of the coming world.[51]

51. For this whole concept and its limitations in comparison with other interpretations, apart from what has already been discussed, see J. Ratzinger, "Herkunft und Sinn der Civitas-Lehre Augustins,"

The fragility inherent in the idea of a Christian world was made clear to Augustine in the year 410, when it was not merely the pagans who clamored for Rome's ancient gods.[52] Hence the state remained for him, in all its real or apparent Christianization, an earthly state, and the Church remained an alien community that accepted and

---

in Congrès International Augustinien, *Augustinus Magister* II (Paris, 1954), 965–79. Although I sought to distinguish my "sacramental" interpretation from the purely eschatological interpretation of W. Kamlah, it is still obvious that, in Augustine's view, the sacramental and the eschatological are complementary. As a *communio caritatis*, the Church remains an alien in this world; it is neither an earthly state nor a theocracy but rather achieves its end at the *eschaton*. To that extent Augustine's sacramental view of the Church maintains rather than does away with an eschatological perspective. That my own interpretation of *The City of God* has been completely misunderstood by U. Duchrow in his *Christenheit und Weltverantwortung* (Stuttgart, 1970), 235–36 should be quite clear from the explanations in the book, which he did not take into consideration (despite the fact that it was available to him). Likewise, A. Wachtel's similar lack of understanding in his *Beiträge zur Geschichtstheologie des Aurelius Augustinus* (Bonn, 1960) could be corrected by considering those explanations.

52. On the position of paganism in the Roman Empire during Augustine's time, see *Bibliothèque Augustinienne* 33, 175–83.

used the earthly but was not at home in it. To be
sure, the coexistence of the two communities was
more peaceful in Augustine's time than it was in
Origen's. Augustine never spoke of plotting against
the "Scythian" state; rather, he felt that it was jus-
tifiable for Christians, who were members of the
eternal homeland, to serve in Babylon as officials
and even as emperors. Thus, while in Origen one
does not see how this world is supposed to keep going but must simply be ready for the breakthrough
of the *eschaton*, Augustine not only counted on the
Roman Empire's continuation but even considered
the empire so central to the world-age in which he
lived that he wished for its renewal. He remained
true to eschatological thinking, however, insofar
as he viewed the whole world as provisional and
consequently did not attempt to give it a Christian
constitution; instead, he let it remain as it was
and allowed it to struggle with its own relative
structure. To that extent the Christianity that was
now lawful by intention was also revolutionary in

an ultimate sense, since it could not be identified with any state but was, rather, a force that relativized everything that was included in the world by pointing to the one absolute God and to the one mediator between God and man, Jesus Christ (1 Tm 2:5).[53]

53. For this reason it is completely erroneous to use the *compelle intrare* of the Donatist struggle to make Augustine the father of the theocratic ecclesiastical constitution of the Middle Ages, even when so-called medieval Augustinianism appealed to him in that regard. The imperial assistance that Augustine hesitatingly accepted against the Donatist partisans known as Circumcellions, and ultimately against the Donatist movement as a whole, neither did away with his basic position regarding the "earthly city" nor, considering the situation, really contradicted it. One cannot rightly make Augustine himself responsible for the false interpretation that was later attached to the Catholic response to Donatism. On the political Augustinianism of the Middle Ages, see H. X. Arqillière, *L'augustinisme politique: essai sur la formation des théories politiques au moyen âge* (Paris, 1956); idem, "Réflexions sur l'essence de l'augustinisme politique," in *Augustinus Magister* II, 991–1002. On Augustine's understanding of the political, see the extensive bibliography in *Bibliothèque Augustinienne* 33, 156–59.

GENERAL INDEX

INDEX OF SCRIPTURAL CITATIONS

INDEX OF SCRIPTURAL CITATIONS